REALIZING
BRAND INDIA

REALIZING
BRAND INDIA

The Changing Face of Contemporary India

Edited by
Sharif D Rangnekar

Photographs Courtesy
Dilip Banerjee

Illustrations Courtesy
E P Unny

Rupa & Co

Published 2005 by

Rupa & Co

7/16, Ansari Road, Daryaganj,
New Delhi 110 002

Sales Centres:

Allahabad Bangalore Chandigarh Chennai
Hyderabad Jaipur Kathmandu
Kolkata Mumbai Pune

Typeset in 11 pts. Memoir by
Nikita Overseas Pvt. Ltd.
1410 Chiranjiv Tower
43 Nehru Place
New Delhi 110 019

Printed and bound in India by
Gopsons Papers Ltd., Noida.

For
Armaan, Aranya and Naveen

CONTENTS

ACKNOWLEDGEMENTS

This book has been a little more than four months in the making from a concept note to a manuscript. Not an easy task given that most of the writers have their own pre-occupations. I thank them all for the support they gave me and for having taken all the pushing during the past few months.

The idea for this book was first shared with Indira Khanna, an external consultant to Rupa & Company who was quick in responding. Had it not been for her acceptance and then of the publishers themselves, the proposed book may not have reached this stage. Thanks — your response has made the book a reality. And Sanjana Roy Choudhury, you have been super.

The assistance from friends has been important to me in putting the book together. I would like to thank Chitra Padmanabhan, M.K. Venu and Munnu Chand for all their inputs for the book and the constant encouragement. Munnu and Venu, in fact, went through the pains of reading through the draft manuscript and providing me with valuable comments that helped me in focusing and improving upon the writings.

There were many who helped me either through thoughts or putting me in touch with some of the brilliant writers who are now part of the book. Khozem Merchant, Kunal Sachdeva, Nitin Mantri, Parul Gossain, Rakesh Thukral, Shivraj Prashad and Sandeepan Deb – thanks for all the help.

Adding an abstract tinge to the book, *The Indian Express* spared its cartoonist E.P. Unny who with his immediate understanding of the theme was a big boost given the paucity of time.

Although the book is not academic in the typical sense, research has played an important role. I thank my team at Indiabiz News & Research Services for all the assistance and Manish Sharma, in particular. My colleagues at Integral PR have also been of assistance. Deepak Talwar and Sanjeev Sharma have been with me all the while. Thanks for the support.

The work has been of late nights and early mornings and often staying away from my routine responsibilities, particularly at home. But an understanding mother, Veena Rangnekar, her wisdom on the subject and a critique too, has been an amazing contribution to this book. My two brothers, Dilip and Dwijen, have also been there through this process and so have been my close family, Sudhir and Rita Kapoor and my aunt in London, Uma Malhotra. And on many nights, to de-stress me (given my work hours), my friends, in particular, Emanuel Joute, have been a source of help in refreshing my mind with quick coffees and reading sessions all of which was fun.

I do hope that the assistance and the efforts have resulted in a book you would cherish.

Sharif D. Rangnekar

NOTE FROM THE EDITOR

One question that has come up on many occasions since work on this book began was why this theme. No one questioned the idea of doing a book and no one ridiculed the theme, but they did wonder whether there was enough substance to justify over a hundred pages.

This is my chance to give a detailed answer. Bear with me.

Till about a year back, I would never have thought of putting together a book on India and that too on its progress, achievements and the contrasts that it offers, which now redefines what the nation means or stands for. I have always been proud of being an Indian but as a typically traditional journalist, have been very careful in admitting what may be a positive development since traditionally, good news did not necessarily make a good report for a newspaper. In effect, being part of the Fourth Estate usually meant looking at the glass half empty, taking upon the role of playing the devils advocate at times and often constructive questioning on the job still to be done. So, suggesting that a part of India is 'shining' and now has led to a changing face or redefinition, could be misconstrued as supportive of campaigns that hijacked the credit from Indian endeavours and entrepreneurship and that the media had been critical of.

This only made this book less probable.

What changed?

It was only the acceptance of the reality that India is on the move. India does not merely stand for a country of snake charmers, elephants, maharajas and palaces. India is not only about poverty, corruption and starvation. India truly has strengths that emphasize the contrasts of a large nation that is exciting, carries great potential and with it, challenges that may take years to address or overcome. This truth is compelling and not to be ignored, I have felt. The successes in India and of Indians to me is as real as the prowess and determination of those who build huge successful businesses, move at the same pace as the developed world and those who struggle for every meal or live in hope that their time is going to come.

There is a new brand, or definition, for India. It stands for a knowledge economy, a growing manufacturing sector, music, art and film, a more articulate player in the global trade scenario, and a growing urban class that is ready to spend more and consume in a manner that till recently was foreign to them.

Taking a broader view, India represents a vibrant economy that is amongst the fastest growing in the world and carries a potential of being an economic superpower in about twenty years from now. The country's economy, significantly, is no more reliant only on a good monsoon that translates into a good performance from the agricultural sector, as the manufacturing and services sector has shown resilience that is a positive indication of what may be in store for the future.

These facts make sense to me and are credible, convincing and as stark a reality as the lack of development in many parts of this nation, beggars on the streets of urban modern India, the struggle for equality for women, child labour or the Gujarat riots that hopefully will go down as a painful aberration of modern Indian history.

An acceptance of the progress and successes is not a denial or intended to cover up for all that is wrong or inappropriate in India. It is merely an acknowledgement that showcases the potential that the country possesses. Unfortunately, a large part of the Indian population tends to put down prosperity or envy it, either because deprivation is rampant or prosperity carries a negative tag. If the aim is to point out the job pending to be done, it is appropriate, but if it is merely to take one down only due to his success, it can be harmful for a nation grappling with a number of issues that needs encouragement rather than discouragement. India is a young nation and most of its history has seen the rule of one king or the other, followed by the dominance of the British. Every ruler was prosperous in a materialistic sense besides being powerful. The ruled only got poorer. This fact has taken a while to get out of the psyche of Indians who were often told that making money is not good, austerity is more important. As a result, Indians for most part of its independent period, have struggled to manage, absorb and accept progress, aspirations, materialism and consumerism.

However, I am not part of that breed but am a section of the changing breed of India.

What made me put together a concept note for this book was a couple of things. Back in 1996, during a visit to Seattle, US, a senior official of a large multinational asked me how I travelled to my place of work. Was it by an elephant, bullock cart or did I walk? My answer, almost offended, was that India was an extremely liberal country full of contrasts that allowed just about any form of transport to survive as long as it had the will and grit to take you from one place to another. So, it could be an elephant, a donkey, a cycle, a scooter, a car or anything else.

I was certainly proud of my answer but it did show a sense of defense and offense since it hurt me to see that India was still perceived as a country of elephants and bullock carts.

In October 2001, when on a holiday in London, I was offered a job with a television channel. I was not interested and this, for some reason, did not go down well with the official of the channel. The person was surprised that I "being an Indian" refused the financial package the channel was ready to pay. The tone was hardly positive and far from pleasant. In fact, there was an under current suggesting that the offer, in money terms, would help me lead a "better" life and no other Indian firm could do the same for me. Hardly did they know!

Obviously, these incidents are still stuck deep within my mind and consciousness. So the changes I see, and possibly many Indians do, does make one proud. It is not that there are jobs available in abundance in India but that Indians are now in a position to negotiate better deals, as they are being recognized and respected for their capability and aptitude. Hence, they have more to chose from today and need not hang on to every international job offer that pops by.

I was thrilled when a well-established close friend of mine called from London saying that he wishes to return to India before the year is out. My eldest brother wants to return to India some time and experience the new work environment. Another friend in the US said that the protectionism and patriotism in that country was unbearable and India is "happening". He is now teaching at the Indian Institute of Management (IIM) in Bangalore. Several other people I know or know off who got pink slips from US information technology companies are now managing the back offices for the same companies from their very own home towns in Hyderabad, Bangalore, Gurgaon and Mumbai.

Following these series of developments was a meeting with a dear journalist friend of mine who works with *The Financial Times*. According to him, there was a growing pressure within the foreign media operating out of the country to produce more stories about India. The curiosity was such that the stories could range from corporate, markets, films, pharmaceutical industry, sports or outsourcing. The pressure has been mounting since October 2003, he had said. This story was no different from the short conversation I had with a journalist working with the *Business Week*.

Email exchanges with a media consultant in the US and then some journalists there, the UK and Singapore, reiterated the same.

This was a marked change and even if I pinched myself, I would not wake up to something else.

India had failed to market or sell itself in the past. The India Brand Equity Fund set up by the government and administered by the ministry of commerce with an objective to "promote Indian Brands in overseas markets" and "make the 'Made in India' label a symbol of quality" at a competitive price, was ineffective. Maybe, the efforts were only to sell an idea or a perceived potential but not a true story that reflects the skills, the knowledge and the possibilities that India possesses. While undoubtedly the picture of unclad, starving children is not yet to be thrown away, this is not the only picture that represents India.

However excited I may feel about our progress as a nation that survives in different periods of time and evolution, I know for sure that India has only made its presence felt and has not "arrived" as yet. Poverty, starvation and corruption continue to plague the country. Cultural differences within the nation are acceptable but economic differences continue to be a challenge.

But I do believe that this is bound to change as the benefits of the reforms process reaches more people. The increasing size of the urban middle class is an indication of the changing India. While this undoubtedly is not representative of the nation at large, efforts are on in different directions to make this change more widespread. India's large golden quadrilateral road project is already under way connecting large parts of the country that with time can lead to creating more hubs for jobs besides reducing the time between cities, towns and villages that are now remote. Large-scale education programmes across every part of the country such as the *Sarva Shiksha Abhiyan* is in place and positive results are already being recorded in many parts where more children are now attending school. Micro-finance has taken off and success stories are already being written not just in India but also in the international media. The current dispensation is in the process of implementing broad based reforms targetting the rural segment as well.

What is more is the small yet significant awakening in urban India that is keen to see other lesser-developed parts of the nation improve. The response to the Gujarat riots and the stories of students of rural development and economics turning down lucrative jobs with foreign firms to work in villages at salaries of just Rs 7,000, is heartening and indicative of the fact that even accomplished students were ready to rough it out to serve the nation and give up a more comfortable life.

What is apparent is that while the literacy level in India may be low, an Indian need not necessarily be considered as unaware or unintelligent. The proliferation of television (there are more television sets in the country than telephones) and the absorption of programming — both entertainment and news — has led to greater awareness and aspirations among Indians at large. The tolerance levels are low as the social and economic distinctions realized by watching television are more pronounced.

The general elections in 2004 marked the entry of economic issues and development as among the key issues that dominated campaigning. A more evolved voter was less interested in religion and more focused on his or her needs that are relevant to survival. The articulation of the electorate and the acceptance by the political class as reflected in the elections is an indication that India is now addressing issues that matter and go beyond hysteria and emotions.

To me, India is evolving and being in the spotlight or a flavour internationally means that the focus is on all that the nation stands for. It is only natural that India is up for scrutiny now and the jury is out. But as its people are not bereft of aspirations, hope, entrepreneurship and will, as they are seeing a realization at least in many quarters, the country is not expected to disappoint.

This could well be the way forward as brand India — the omnipotent elephant — places its foot on the global map.

Cheers!

FOREWORD

Over the last few years, India has increasingly become the "flavour of the day" with influential sections of the foreign media, some foreign policy establishments, adventurous tourists and even stock market investors. Instead of being perceived as a dirty, over-populated country of poor and illiterate people, India is increasingly considered a land of opportunity with intelligent, motivated and technically-skilled people. Many factors have contributed to this image make-over, this transition from a land of starvation and spirituality to one of surging stock-markets and bright brains. The Information Technology industry is certainly one of them, as are India's growing technological prowess — especially in space and nuclear technologies — and its steady economic growth. These are certainly based on solid performance; yet, the "India Shining" campaign of the previous government had at least a few doubters.

As anyone who has even a cursory knowledge of India will confirm, whatever one says about India is true, and so is its opposite. This yin and yang, this continual contradiction, holds with regard to the India Shining issue too. On the one hand, large sections of urban India are undoubtedly enjoying levels of prosperity and consumption that are way beyond what their parents experienced. The pubs of Bangalore and the malls of Gurgaon bear evidence to this as much as the influx of new cars in Ludhiana or Ahmedabad. Indicators like sales of motorcycles, airline traffic, housing loans, and restaurant sales are all going through the roof. Hordes of Indians are holidaying abroad and tens of thousands are going to foreign universities, as full-fee paying students. Some part of India seems to have become a developed nation.

On the other hand, destitution continues for a large segment of the population. Women yet walk kilometers to collect drinking water and firewood. Suicides by farmers facing financial ruin due to droughts are yet taking place. Caste and gender discrimination has not gone away, nor have T.B, malaria and other sicknesses. Slums continue to proliferate, even as they are occasionally demolished, and all forms of urban degradation are visible even in the shiny metropolises of new India.

Dreams and despair, apathy and activism, poverty and prosperity continue to co-exist side by side in India's great tradition of tolerance. No synthesis has yet emerged from the dialectics of thesis and antithesis.

India has had its opulent feudal class and the rich zamindar. It has also seen the wealthy trader and industrialist, and the conspicuous consumption of the capitalist. The one change in recent years has been the upsurge of middle-class prosperity, creating a strange new tribe of "rich middle-class". It is this that signifies a discontinuity, a radical re-orientation of Indian society. This class, though small, has bought the dreams of globalization and been instrumental in catalyzing the liberalization and opening-up of India. It sees the rest of the world not as a potential threat — the paradigm of the Independence generation — but as a market. Many of these people are technical professionals, retaining many traditional middle-class values, but now have a new sense of self-confidence that marks them out as different. They feel that they can take on the world and compete with all comers; in some sectors — like IT — they have shown that this is not mere bravado.

However, the poor, backward India has not disappeared. Some parts of rural India yet live in centuries long gone by, while many parts of urban India live in such squalor that it challenges notions of the ambience required for human survival.

Connections between these two Indias are tenuous and are in desperate need of strengthening. The first step must be a better understanding of the issues, needs and possible means of solving problems. Many of the economic issues have, as their root cause, poor governance, policy/strategic direction, and structural issues. Without early correction of the pitfalls, there is real danger to the sustainability of this model of development, and indeed to this form of governance. For a country long steeped in apathy and brainwashed into deterministic theories of "karma", this may seem like a strong statement; yet, grass-roots observations bear this out. The dark side of the Moon cannot be long neglected.

Greater discussion and debate on the state of the economy, polity and society are essential. An analysis of the situation, context and alternative perspectives on issues are all necessary parts of this. It is in this context that one welcomes this attempt to bring together the perspectives of respected commentators from diverse fields, to look at how India is doing, whether it is shining and the path ahead.

Kiran Karnik
President, Nasscom
September 2004

INTRODUCTION

It was in the midst of the Indian monsoon of 1991, July 24 to be precise, that the then finance minister and now the prime minister of India, Dr. Manmohan Singh, decided to direct the Indian economic policy into a path it had tried to avoid for several years. Dr. Singh, on this historic day, proclaimed that India would open its doors to foreign direct investment (FDI). He indicated then that India would slowly remove barriers that disallowed the involvement of foreign entities in the functioning of corporate India and the nation's economy. He also stated that a series of structural reforms were on the cards, including doing away with the numerous bureaucratic hurdles that the private sector had to experience while trying to get a permit to do just about anything relevant to the running of a business.

There was more to come as Dr. Singh went about his business designing what was, and is now known as, economic reforms.

The world was watching then and acknowledged Dr. Singh's intentions but somehow was not too convinced about how the process would map out given India's democracy and predominantly socialistic background. The foreign perception was not misplaced as the nation was confused and divided. While the necessity for the reforms was not always understood, what was often questioned was the conviction and the political will of the then Congress regime. The party was the oldest Indian political party and was an integral part of India's freedom movement and independence from foreign rule. Since Independence in 1947, India had focused on self-dependence and sufficiency and a minimal, if not nil, space for the Western world. With this distinct history and mission in mind, the integrity of the government was always under question.

Had the government sold out?

Is India up for sale?

Can't India be self-sufficient?

Was a foreign agenda being run through the Indian government?

These questions were common during the monsoon of 1991, and the debate over economic reforms came up almost every time Indian policy makers and industry struggled to adjust and assess the direction of change. But then Indians had every reason to question the system that had fostered and nurtured inefficiency, austerity over prosperity and an increasing population that survived till death searching for a square meal and maybe, if given a chance, some clothing to clad themselves. The Indian approach was generally not to aim high, as prosperity was for the corrupt and powerful (the residual effect of the British Raj and a section of the rich class), so austerity was more acceptable.

But Dr. Singh was sure that India could not live in history and had to recognize and accept the ground realities. The nation was starved of foreign exchange and at the same time was cradled with huge foreign debt and almost no way to pay it back, besides an inflation rate that the Indian social make up or for that matter in most other nations, would term as painfully difficult to live with.

India, being the democracy it is, the reforms process often went off track and at times, almost stalled as populism played a huge role when it came to elections. Even Dr. Singh had to tone down his economic agenda as the Congress government prepared for the elections they lost. But even as each party argued between and within themselves, there was unanimity that the process started would carry on even if it lacked pace.

Significantly, even coalition governments felt that reforms could not be reversed although seemingly difficult to impose, since the results were not apparent to a large part of India. By 1998, the desperate need for cheap funds, jobs, entrepreneurship and administrative reforms was still a stark reality.

Still, the Indian government did the unthinkable that summer — ran nuclear tests (May 21, 1998). Coming from a country that was grappling with several domestic issues, the nuclear tests seemed completely misplaced and an expense that the economy could hardly afford. While most of the Indian media responded cautiously to begin with, the national English press came down heavily against the historic and contentious tests.

The moot point then was whether India needed to conduct the tests. Should a poor country like India spend huge sums on a nuclear programme that only prepared for war rather than peace? Would the tests lead to war and greater instability in the region given that India and China were not necessarily on the best of terms? Did India need to display supremacy?

The questions were endless and the responses always had a counter clearly indicating that the nation and its people were caught between the economic impact of the tests, a show of strength and nationalism.

At that point, the arguments against the test were valid when purely examining the ground realities of the state of the Indian economy, unemployment, poverty, starvation and other forms of deprivation. The economic reforms process was also losing pace at that time and the benefits were not necessarily very visible. The nuclear tests, as per news reports, cost India several thousand crores and for all the starving, tax paying and deprived people of the country, this was a lot of money that could have translated into food, jobs and greater opportunities.

The international community at large reacted in shock and dismay. Prior to this, India was always viewed a pretender, posturing more often than seeming even to be slightly threatening. The country's track record was such that it was considered a soft nation living in the past, grappling with poverty and a bureaucracy that did not move, contributing to a system that bred corruption. This being the case, complacency was all that the world outside the country expected of the country. So, a nuclear test by India was far from anyone's imagination.

India was clearly seen as an offender creating a situation of increased instability in the region. India's relationship with China was not friendly, Pakistan was a traditional foe and the verbal friction between these two nations had resulted in foreign investors always putting a high political risk rating for the region. The world over there were all kinds of fears that war could break out between Pakistan and India. However, Pakistan did not go to that extent and followed India's nuclear tests with its own.

By then, India had already faced the ire of many nations. The US had decided to impose economic sanctions on India and countries like Japan and the UK did not waste much time in following suit. India stated that it had already allowed for some economic response, but was willing to take the consequences. Several sectors where the import of technology was imperative such as chemicals, computers, telecommunication, construction and automobiles, were bound to face the impact of strict sanctions. What India hoped for was that the presence of American multinationals in some of these sectors would lead to the US government reconsidering the severity of the sanctions.

At that point, India owed a total of US $ 44 billion in loans and had provided for just US $6 billion in repayment to the International Monetary Fund (IMF) and the World Bank. Corporate India was looking towards raising debt abroad but the sanctions meant fewer options and also higher interest costs given the political risk factor following the nuclear tests. In fact, the US credit rating agency, Moodys, pointed out that a reduction of capital flows, including direct investments and debt, "could not come at a worse time", arguably one of the largest credit rating agencies, since India's economic reforms programme was now off track. Standard and Poors, however, felt that the sanctions would have a limited impact given that the Indian economy was insular in nature and the role of foreign investment was small.

This was certainly a low for the nation but it did have some positive results that seem to have a strong connection with the India of today. Economic sanctions and the ridiculing of India the world over resulted in the non-resident Indian (NRI) population rallying behind its country and connecting with its own back home. The response to the Resurgent India Bonds (RIBs) was one such example of how Indians felt. Even the urban Indian and national media felt that the nation was being slighted by larger powers that had already conducted their own set of tests in the past. Being done in was what a large part of the aware Indians felt and the general thought was that international response had little to do with peace and more to do with envy. Even if this were not entirely true, Indians did feel a sense of pride that extended to nationalism.

The year 1998, in fact, marked the rolling out of the second phase of economic reforms. The National Democratic Alliance (NDA) government decided to raise the levels of foreign equity in different sectors, further simplified the approval process, decided to remove certain administrative red tape for domestic corporations besides a series of other initiatives including identifying the information technology sector as a priority sector, as the then prime minister, Atal Behari Vajpayee told the Indian Economic Summit in November that year.

He followed this initiative directed to the international community and media with yet another one. This was pure politics. Vajpayee went ahead with the Lahore Bus *yatra* (ride) that the world received as a significant peace-making effort. At that point, the world did expect reducing tension between the traditional foes.

But by the summer of 1999, cross border tension with Pakistan was at a high and a limited war in Kargil was already under way. The fear then was that a full-scale war was a possibility and the world was watching which way matters would progress. The government used the television media effectively to send pictures to all the relevant nations of Indian soldiers suffering. These pictures (part of India's diplomacy) and the decision to play the role of the defender, in this instance, were well received across the globe. The war may have meant a huge expense and increased taxes, but nationalism was on the rise and the recognition of India's posture for peace internationally made Indians prouder than they were. As a result, tax surcharges were insignificant to even the urban class that always found their take home reducing due to taxes.

Moreover, the Kargil war, in a very limited way, had vindicated India's position on the nuclear tests.

This all sounded good but even over eight years into the reforms programme, India had little to write home about other than the nuclear tests, the Lahore bus and war diplomacy, Professor Amartya Sen's achievement of winning the Nobel Prize for Economics and the listing of Infosys and Wipro on US stock exchanges. 9/11 only emphasized the fact that India was hardly on the radar of the international community, including the US. The international media, for example, hardly gave any significance to India's response condemning the act even as lesser-developed nations hogged column centimeters. In fact, it was noted in some sections of the press here that it was not until the seventh day after 9/11 that India figured in the leading publications in the US, and that seemed more as a second thought.

If India did get any significant mention, it was much later after the terrorist attacks on the Indian Parliament that emphasized the need and relevance of the US government's contentious war against terrorism drive. But this incident and the publicity that followed, led to questions on how safe the country was in terms of living, visiting and investing. This meant, yet again, that India had to go through its economic issues on its own without any sizeable foreign support. However, as put by a top corporate executive, India was already getting used to such situations, so it was better prepared after the Parliament attacks than after the nuclear tests.

However, at that time, India did not know that it was turning a corner. Between 2002 and now, India made advances in several areas and an India flavour and fragrance could be tasted and sniffed in different parts of the world.

Consider this.

The Silicon Valley had become a little India. Multinationals were preferring Indian techies because of their skills and lower costs. Business Process Outsourcing (BPO) was not just a huge business due to the role that India and Indians were playing, but was also a key topic of debate in the US since it had meant taking away jobs to hubs in Bangalore, Gurgaon, Mumbai, Hyderabad and smaller towns such as Jaipur and Pune.

Indian cinema made a mark when *Lagaan* was nominated for an Oscar in 2002. Aishwarya Rai, a former Miss World and now a leading heroine, a year later was part of the Cannes Film Festivals team of judges besides making it to the *Time* magazine cover. In 2004, the film *Kal Ho Na Ho* made it to the Oscar archives. Indian entrepreneurship could be seen not just in the manufacturing sector that was out shopping for foreign firms, but also in individuals who did not get deterred by pink slips in the US as they returned to serve, at times, the same companies through the outsourcing route.

Indians were now a proud people enjoying the limelight that they never had, at least for positive reasons. The recognition from across the seas has made Indians less shy of themselves. The mere fact that an American accent is not picked up in a few days (obviously, barring the call center folks servicing the US who are trained to speak in a certain manner), as was the case some years ago, is a sure sign of the new Indians who are proud of what they are.

India's urban class is also a contributor to the pride, flavour and redefinition of the nation. The ease with which Indians swipe credit and debit cards to shop and consume is a growing trend that has also led to the development of the retail segment. Urban Indians, in many ways, now have a lifestyle that is closer to their counterparts in other parts of the world. And growing consumerism is replacing austerity and constantly redefining what luxury stands for.

With the advent of television and advertising, the Indian is better informed and aware of his rights and needs. While consumerism is an indication, the behavior of the electorate is another, where a large part of India now knows what it is missing.

With these elements, the nation's economy shifted gears in 2003-04 notching up a 10.4 per cent growth rate for the third quarter. Its ability to manage trade issues appeared more certain, and the prospects in the future seem greater than ever.

Think of it. Is this what India was a few years ago? No, is the simplest and closest-to-truth answer. However, one could say that India always had the potential but did not show its ability to realize it. But now the change is there to see and what has possibly influenced India's belief in itself is not just the realization of its ability but the acknowledgement from quarters that are perceived as progressive achievers that Indians at large have looked up to — right or wrong.

The foreign media, for example, has not stopped examining and reporting on just what has happened in a country that has always reflected complacency and the inability to get a move on. The intrigue is even greater given that India is taking strides at a time when FDIs have been dipping and are hardly above the US $ 2 billion-mark for 2003-04.

Such facts and success stories in different areas have led to a curiosity that was earlier limited to poverty – a terribly ugly part of India that much of the developed world has been distant from for several decades, heritage, history and corruption.

*R*ealizing *Brand India* takes you through the India story and maps out the key drivers of the perception change during the recent past, the India flavour abroad, the many Indias that exist within this vast nation and the potential that can keep the evolution going.

The uniqueness of this book is that it brings together a variety of journalists, analysts and writers who have been tracking India's progress both domestically and internationally. They carry on-ground knowledge of what India is, how it functions, what its people are like, the cultural differences, the contrasts and much more.

The book does not intend to pay a tribute or gloss over the positives, and ignore the fact that India continues to struggle with the reform process and the need to have a broad-based approach that includes the farm sector and addresses hunger and poverty.

What it does is recognize Brand India, realize its potential and what it stands for today.

Even as I write these lines and the book goes through the necessary process relevant to its ultimate publication, India, the nation, may have moved that much ahead in its constant discovery of potential and challenges that has so many versions, which when strung together create an attractive and exciting necklace that can embrace just about anyone.

For the writers, commentators and analysts who have contributed to the book and possibly for many millions of people and I, India has changed and will continue to as the nation and the people evolve.

Sharif D. Rangnekar
New Delhi
September, 2004

THE BEGINNING
OF THE ARRIVAL

The other day, at one of those Page 3 parties, a group claimed that India had 'arrived' on the international scene. I immediately turned my head and realized that this feeling was almost unanimous within that specific group. Gosh, was I shocked that the basis of the conclusion was that a disco in New York City had a bhangra night and so India had arrived!

There are many who believe that a nomination for an Oscar or fusion music efforts are sufficient to generate recognition and acceptance in a larger sense. Indian music maybe appreciated and so could be Hindi films, but that's just a small part of India that hardly represents the nation.

What is often forgotten is that only a string of events diverse in nature and sustainable can contribute to a changed perception, a redefinition or possibly the 'arrival' of a nation in the loose sense, on the global map. And what is often the key to sustaining a nation are not just the frills — it is a strong economy, potential, and more than that, the conviction, will and the skills to move on and tap what is and what can be.

Roopa Purushothaman, in her own way has penned down the nation's achievements and potential into an appropriate perspective that assists in defining where the nation stands today and how it may evolve in the time to come.

The Change

I think the private sector is driving a lot of the fundamental changes in the economy. Globally, competitive firms are raising the bar for governance and productivity. We are still in the early stages of this process, which can still go either way, but as more competition develops we hope to see larger private sector opportunities, which could lead the way for areas such as labour market development.

At the same time, we are seeing a sea change in public support for the reform process, which means that reforms no longer have to be done 'in stealth'. Politically, it has become more acceptable to implement reform policies, which hopefully means that the process will continue and eventually will be able to integrate the economy across geographies, such as the rural to the urban economy, allowing access for previously isolated areas to larger production networks.

India's services-led growth strategy could continue to benefit from domestic as well as global demand, providing a sustainable growth driver for the future.

The Strengths and Pitfalls in the Indian Economy

In each of the 'conditions for growth' we lay out in the paper[1], India has both strengths and weaknesses. For instance, with regard to macroeconomic policy, India's steering of monetary and foreign exchange policy has been a source of strength, while the fiscal deficit remains a significant burden. In looking at political institutions, India has a sound political structure and functioning judiciary, despite inefficiencies.

However, bureaucracy and excessive regulation still weigh down the economy. In terms of openness, the country has made significant strides to open the economy so that trade, as a share of the Gross Domestic Product (GDP), is now roughly double its level in the early 1980s. The pace of opening the economy has had its benefits. However, the economy is still relatively closed to trade and investment against most of the other BRICs (as an example). In education, which I discuss below, India has

---

[1] Goldman Sachs' Global Economics Paper No: 99, Dreaming With BRICs: The Path to 2050.

seen significant success in tertiary education, but more needs to be done at the levels of basic education.

Competition to China

If India continues with its reform programme and concentrates on ensuring broader development across the board, India could be 'the next China'. However, India's specialization in services is in stark contrast to China's manufacturing tilt. Because India is about ten to fifteen years behind China in its reforms, you could see the 'sweet spot' for growth as yet to come in India.

While India's growth could be stronger than China's over the long run, the size of China's economy would still be larger.

Steps to be Taken

I would highlight three key areas. First, education needs to be made more broad-based. Primary and secondary education needs to reach a larger share of the population in order to realize a real strengthening in human capital, which has intricate value in itself as well as being the key to sustaining services-led growth.

Second, momentum in infrastructure building needs to continue. We have seen real progress in recent years, but India has to ensure that networks between urban centers as well as crucially between rural and urban settings develop. The country is starting from such a low infrastructure base, that increased access to larger production networks will allow for sizeable gains in the private sector.

Third, the labour sector needs to be made more flexible. Unemployment is a serious issue, the creation of a formal labour sector is still in the very early stages given the size of the labour force, and the country will need a labour market that will be able to absorb structural and sectoral changes in the economy.

The Perception

India now stands for more than just history, culture, poverty and heritage. To the global community, and this is just anecdotally, I think the perception of India has tangibly changed over the past year.

Although the IT sector is still such a small part of the economy, the fact that it has had such an impact on trade and migration has played a significant role in changing perceptions and interactions. Migration, especially, has been key to this shift. Many more people outside the country are clamouring to gain an insight into understanding the country, and the interest has gathered steadily over the past year.

Still, I think the idea of Brand India is in its infancy and will evolve over the years. Globally, the perception seems to be that India has some serious strengths in its labour force, its specialization in services — which has the flavor of India developing in its own way, a departure from manufacturing-led growth seen across the region historically.

However, the question of whether this is for real, rather than a cyclical blip on the back of good monsoons is a concern. Poverty, caste dynamics, and communalism are continuing complex issues. India's always had the potential, but now we are at the stage of hoping that it can actually realize this potential and make a departure from the disappointments in the past.

DRIVING A PERCEPTION CHANGE

THE IT SECTOR

The India story, it is strongly believed, began with the advent of the nation's Information Technology segment. It is in this sector that India arguably has made its greatest impression and the ink is still wet and whatever has dried, is for sure indelible. The strange bit about this story that virtually put India on the international map has been the subtle manner in which this nation's people made inroads into the businesses and lives of the developed world, particularly the United States.

Indians and knowledge were not necessarily expected to go hand-in-hand. Indians playing a role to improve efficiencies of large business houses and multinationals outside the nation's shores was, yet again, not part of the globalization script, in that, it was not a certainty as such that India would assume a significant role. And given India's efficiency levels, the Indian IT story was almost a contradiction. That Indians would know more and determine how the efficiencies of businesses would improve or how the people of this nation would reduce operational costs and increase profit margins for many multinational organizations, was possibly what the doctor ordered, but not a foregone conclusion until it started to happen.

India's rise in the global scenario is intriguing and peculiar. Its software and services exports industry accounts for about two per cent of worldwide spending, as Goldman Sachs' (GS)[1]

[1] Golman Sachs' Global Economic Paper Number 109 by Roopa Purushothman, April 14, 2004.

points out. What explains the hype then? The mere performance and potential that India holds in a world where the IT skill sets available are depleting, makes India significant and Indians sought after. The GS economic paper suggests "India's IT services exports benefited from a comparative advantage in knowledge workers with a specific set of software and language skills."

These skills came in handy also to create the nation's growing business process outsourcing (BPO) segment. Its great advantage, particularly in the area of call centers, has been the English speaking abilities in India. India has the second largest English speaking population outside Britain, after the Americans. These founding factors aside, what India does is bring down costs for foreign firms. According to a review study by Nasscom [2], the cost of personnel in India is fourteen per cent less than in the US. Telecommunication costs are lower by 155 per cent and rentals are cheaper by a third. In addition, depreciation laws in India are fifty per cent more beneficial.

Points out Professor Kaushik Basu of Cornell University, "the unprecedented collaboration with India's information technology, in the form of both admitting computer scientists in Silicon Valley and outsourcing work to India, gave the US the competitive edge."[3] This may explain why some US multinationals rallied behind outsourcing and in fact set up their own units in India, making sure that the benefits remain within their global operations.

Consider this. Of the total revenues earned by this industry, 38 per cent is cornered by MNCs even as they own just about 5 per cent of the 400-odd BPOs[4]. No wonder, India's BPO segment has players such as General Electric, HSBC, J P Morgan Chase and Standard Chartered, to name a few.

Indian companies also seem to be looked as promising investments. Infosys and Wipro are said to have been well

---

[2] The Nasscom Strategic Review 2003.
[3] Posted on Outsourcing News from the article 'Outsourcing: Long term gains for all', March 26, 2004.
[4] IT-ITES in India, May 2004 — Indiabiz News And Research Services.

received when listed on Nasdaq and more recently, eDaksh Services, one of India's bigger BPOs, was taken over by IBM.

To Indians in India, the sector has lent to pride and a belief that India is not necessarily dependent as they service the needs of the world and is being seen as the global hub for back offices. Even if this is exaggerated and the need is mutual, it is clear that India's presence on the globe has a lot to do with the success of the nation's IT professionals and language skills that the education system has nurtured.

Going beyond merely the sector and its related enabling services, IT in many ways, has built the starting block for the new global Indian agenda, where heads of state pay searching visits to Bangalore's IT campuses, where meek programmers from Hyderabad and Bangalore are seen as Ninja warriors, stalking corridors, plucking out jobs from cubicles next to you, in offices spanning from sunny Sao Paulo to gloomy Blackpool. IT has given good old manufacturing and all forms of Indian products and services a solid leg-up. The IT wave has also heralded, for many Indian corporations, in many ways the seamless transition from liberalization to globalization.

Indian businesses thus benefit from the best of many worlds; a strong India service brand, an environment, which allows them to prowl around more freely than ever before and the highest levels of self-confidence and faith that they have ever

The Indian Back Office Towns

felt and experienced, at least in the last three decades. And of course, a truly information empowered society.

It is expected that the IT and IT services could contribute as much as ten per cent of the Indian gross domestic product (GDP) alone and this has a lot to do with the trend in exports (up 20.4 per cent in 2002-03 and up again by over 30 per cent in 2003-04) and the expected proliferation of outsourcing units in the country. Besides, the revenues of the back office and call centre companies are mounting. According to Nasscom, revenues grew 46 per cent to US $3.6 billion for third party companies and were expected to grow by 40 per cent in the current financial year to March 2005. This would mean crossing the US $5 billion level.

Forget the positive rippling effect. The significance of this sector is so great that the GS report quoted earlier says: "India may have missed the wave of labour-intensive manufactured exports that contributed to growth across much of East Asia, but it will now be able to create a parallel process with labour-intensive software and IT services."

But where did the story begin? How did India take advantage of its strength? Where to from now? Is India ready to move up a level?

The following chapter takes you through these questions and answers them and puts them into perspective.

ENABLING THE WORLD

R. Venkatraman

India's visibility and that of Indians in the global arena has been steadily increasing over the last couple of decades. The frequency with which India gets written about in the print media and gets discussed on TV shows is at unprecedented levels, particularly over the past two years or so. While a good portion of this is due to geopolitical considerations, a large part of this new visibility stems from what India, as a country, has to offer to global businesses — either as a market or as a resource base. The number of foreign business travellers coming to India has skyrocketed. One has only to spend ten minutes at Bangalore airport at peak hour to be convinced of this.

How did this all come about?

Let us take a brief moment to trace the developments in the last two decades.

The 'IT (Information Technology) Boom', as we like to call it, started about twenty years ago. We started off in a small way by taking advantage of the acute global shortage of IT skills. We discovered that we were particularly good at IT, specially our young graduates. Indian IT companies sensed a huge business opportunity here and were very quick to seize it. Thus, started the 'body shopping' era of the IT boom. It was the logical thing to do at that point in time when the Indian IT companies did not have the contacts and the wherewithal to take advantage of the opportunity in any other way. Attracted by global career opportunities, many of our bright young minds opted for this. Once these people landed in foreign lands and started working there, their high quality of work was there for everyone to see.

The rest, as they say, is history.

Indian IT professionals successfully transitioned from 'skilled bodies' to high-quality technicians and to successful entrepreneurs. Many went further and became highly successful investors and venture capitalists. While the Silicon Valley was the centre of this transition, it quickly spread to most parts of the United States and then to Europe.

I remember a conversation I had in the 1980s that would be quite unimaginable now. I was the only Indian at an IT seminar in Atlanta. A senior executive from a New York-based IT firm, on being told that I was an Indian, took me to be a Native American Indian. When I tried to correct this impression, I was surprised to learn that he had never heard of a country called India, and had no idea where it was!

Completely unimaginable today. I am sure many IT professionals of my age group would have similar incidents to narrate.

One outstanding quality of Indians (at least in the younger folk) is the ability to adapt quickly to foreign cultures, especially at the workplace. We have been good at blending into any local work culture, while preserving our 'Indian-ness' away from work. Therefore, while Indian professionals have been very successful at work, they were also able to create 'Little Indias' around themselves away from work. And this went a very long way in increasing the visibility of India around the globe. Indian culture and cuisine has taken root in many, many places in different countries.

India has now become an integral part of the IT world. Seldom can you go to an IT company, or the IT department of any reasonable sized company, and not meet an Indian. Every IT conference worth its name will have Indians participating. The combination of sound technical skills and high adaptability to foreign cultures has made Indian IT professionals acceptable around the globe. In many places in the world, the face of India is a young IT professional.

While the 'IT Boom' started two decades ago, many Indians had been migrating to foreign countries (particularly the US) well before that. They have been going abroad for higher studies for a long time. Many Indians who migrated overseas twenty or thirty years ago now find themselves in positions where they can influence thinking and decision-making. This is particularly so in the corporate sector. Therefore, it is no surprise that global corporations are now sitting up and taking notice of India.

India is now being viewed both as a place for resources — particularly human resource — as well as a promising market (we are a country of more than a billion people!). No global corporation can now afford to ignore India. If they do so, it is at their own cost.

In addition to being a country of more than a billion people, it is a place that has seen very high growth rates — be it in mobile phones, consumer financing or any other area. India's attraction goes beyond its size and demonstrated growth. Market penetration of many goods and services is very low. Per capita consumption is close to the bottom of the pile in many instances. Therefore, the promise is huge, and this makes India a 'must be' market for many. They still need to work out market access mechanisms and pricing strategies, but the promise is apparent.

India has firmly established its presence in the global business arena. To some it is a huge opportunity, and to some it is a threat. And to many, it is both. History teaches us that this is to be expected. Any 'new arrival' on the global scene creates such a situation, and we should expect resistance. It would be naïve on our part not to do so. Whether we look at it globally or within our own country, we find that the entry of a new player generates resistance from those who believe that they have something to lose and optimism in those who may stand to gain.

The current wave of protests against outsourcing in the US should be seen in this context. It is but a manifestation of resistance to a new player, to a new offering. Statistically, the number of jobs being outsourced may not be significant, but the mere thought of jobs moving away makes some people uncomfortable. It is an emotional thing. It is an ideal emotional peg for politicians to hang a hat on during an election year. Again, this is something we need to expect and address with maturity. The good thing for India is that the captains of US industry see outsourcing as an opportunity and not as a threat. As do business leaders in Europe. It makes business sense. Outsourcing is a fundamental shift in how businesses are managed. It will happen despite political opposition.

If this is so, and if there is going to be a huge demand for outsourcing services (IT services, BPO, call centres, design services, etc), what is India doing to make sure that this demand can be met? What are the government and the outsourcing industry doing to ensure that we do not have supply side hurdles? The two supply-side areas that are being worked upon are infrastructure and human resources.

The government is looking at various policy measures and enablers to ensure that these do not become hurdles. The good thing is that these measures are being taken well before infrastructure and human resources become bottlenecks. The industry players are working with the government and among themselves to do whatever it takes to ensure that the demand can indeed be captured. Several potential opportunities in different industry sectors have been wasted in the past due to inappropriate measures or inadequate action. This time around, it promises to be different with the government and the industry working closely together.

Here is a brief sketch of what is being contemplated and initiated.

A number of states across the country are initiating policy measures and investing in infrastructure that will aid IT and outsourcing activity.

Typical measures taken by several states are focused on investments related to telecom infrastructure through private sector partnerships, issuing specific ITeS policies besides investing in English language schools and basic computer education for all students. This is in addition to increased encouraged involvement of the private sector in IteS-specific training and testing certification.

Nasscom and KPMG recently conducted a study on the supply side readiness of several states in India. The study assesses thirteen locations across India on various parameters relating to infrastructure and human resources, and comments on their readiness to take advantage of the potentially huge demand for outsourcing services. The study suggests that most locations swing between a focus on infrastructure development

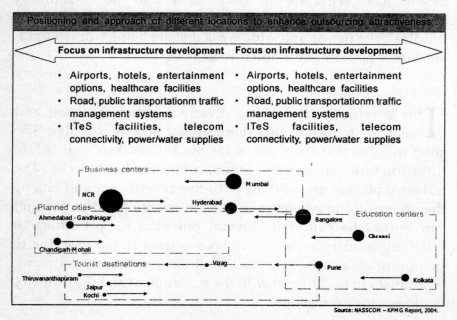

Positioning and approach of different locations to enhance outsourcing attractiveness

Focus on infrastructure development   Focus on infrastructure development

• Airports, hotels, entertainment options, healthcare facilities
• Road, public transportationm traffic management systems
• ITeS facilities, telecom connectivity, power/water supplies

• Airports, hotels, entertainment options, healthcare facilities
• Road, public transportationm traffic management systems
• ITeS facilities, telecom connectivity, power/water supplies

Business centers — NCR — Mumbai
Planned cities — Ahmedabad - Gandhinagar — Hyderabad — Bangalore — Education centers
Chandigarh-Mohali — Chennai
Tourist destinations — Vizag — Pune
Thiruvananthapuram — Jaipur — Kochi — Kolkata

Source: NASSCOM – KPMG Report, 2004.

(e.g. providing facilities for outsourcing, providing telecom and power supply, improving quality of life) and a focus on HR development (e.g. providing specialized skills training, generating pool of educated resources). As can be seen from the earlier graphic, locations are at different points in the 'infrastructure — human resources' spectrum, and are moving in one direction or the other. The locations that are already strong on the infrastructure front are focusing their efforts on improving human resources, and vice-versa.

One also finds that these locations fall into four different groups. Firstly, there are the 'Business Centers' like the National Capital Region (NCR — Delhi, Gurgaon and Noida) and Mumbai that have benefited from the availability of business infrastructure and pool of employable people. Then there are the 'Education Centers' such as Kolkata and Chennai. These have invested in a robust education institutional infrastructure but have traditionally seen skills migrate to other places. Such locations are now investing in infrastructure and marketing efforts to attract outsourcing related investments. The third group comprises the 'tourism destinations' like Jaipur and Kochi, which can leverage their service orientation and associated infrastructure (like hotels, transportation services). These locations are now investing in developing human resources. And finally, there are the 'planned cities' like Chandigarh that have been systematically investing in infrastructure. They too are now investing in improving human resources and skills. They hope to attract anchor investors while developing a pool of skilled resources.

Within the broad groups of 'infrastructure' and 'human resources' there are a number of elements. For example, there under infrastructure, you have connectivity, power, accessibility (roads, airport), business continuity arrangements, etc, which further break down into sub-elements. Connectivity, for example, is not the same for voice (e.g. call centers) and non-voice (e.g. BPO) operations. Similarly, the skill requirements for voice and non-voice are different. And within non-voice, there are industry or function specific skills such as insurance or accounting or engineering design.

An interesting outcome of this is that different locations actually offer different combinations of supply-side elements. Once one digs below the surface, one finds that different locations offer different propositions to potential outsourcers. Depending on what you want to do in the area of outsourcing, you may find one location more appropriate than others.

Another way of looking at this is that states really do not need to compete against each other by offering similar propositions. Instead of competing, they can actually collaborate. By offering different combinations of supply-side elements, they can, in a sense, 'specialise' within the IT and outsourcing area. This way the country can offer a spectrum of choices to potential outsources and outsourcing into India can be maximized.

Over and above the existing infrastructure and skills, specific state governments are putting in place different policy measures and making targeted investments to further enhance the attractiveness of different Indian cities for outsourcing. For example, a number of the states are now looking at putting place policies and mechanisms to ensure data privacy. Details of the various locations, what they offer and their initiatives are available in the Nasscom-KPMG report.

In addition to the various measures being taken by state governments, there is evidence of a clear intent to support the outsourcing industry by the Central government. The recent announcement permitting call centers to use the same infrastructure for overseas as well as domestic business is a step in the right direction.

Acknowledging the need to expand into newer areas in outsourcing and realising that human resources can potentially become a bottleneck, the Central government constituted an industry-oriented task force to examine the issue in detail. This can be seen as a serious move to further increase India's competitive advantage in the outsourcing industry. Specifically, the task force was asked to:

- Delineate a strategy for enhancing the institutional capacity in formal and non-formal education sectors;
- Identify emerging areas in the knowledge domain where India can acquire and retain comparative advantage;
- Suggest policy measures to maximise private participation; and
- Prepare an implementation plan.

Based on the findings of the task force, several measures are to be initiated that take into account the entire education lifecycle.

There include setting up of an 'Awareness Fund' to attract people especially from the Tier II and Tier III cities, promoting foreign languages (French, German, etc), certification using industry-standard tests, reforming labour laws to support part-time and temporary employment, and providing tax relief for IT equipment for people working from home. The recent announcement allowing call centres to utilise equipment for domestic and overseas business was one of the measures envisaged that has already been implemented.

Of these measures, the one relating to certification and standardisation of training can have a significant positive impact. This envisages a central agency that will set standards, administer & oversee training and certify quality of manpower. Currently, a very significant part of an IT or outsourcing company's costs relate to training. If basic training and certification gets done at an industry level, IT and outsourcing companies can become more efficient and competitive.

All in all, it appears that India's role in the global arena will continue to increase. The government and the outsourcing industry appear to be doing the right things to make this happen and it appears that this process will continue for some more years.

Once that happens, the change will be permanent and irreversible.

INDIAN INDUSTRY

India and manufacturing — seemingly at two ends of a line where the two would never meet. This was a common refrain that reflected a lack of belief and self-confidence that India could actually have a manufacturing sector to talk about. This belief had its basis on the fact that this nation was, and possibly still is, primarily an agricultural economy. India's comparative advantage in global trade would also revolve around the farm sector and its produce and not on the corporate manufacturing sector. So went the belief.

Yet, a lot of emphasis was laid on the reforms required to build a vibrant manufacturing sector that could provide the domestic market with goods and possibly, a presence in the export market at some stage. This was so much what India wanted and aspired for. After all, the West's development was more about industry and industrial revolution rather than agriculture. In fact, agriculture was seen as basic and not progressive and therefore not a sign of development. The government initiated all sorts of administrative reforms and reduced import tariffs on capital goods that assisted the corporate sector. Lower interest rates also meant cheaper money to invest in plants and machinery.

But these measures and many more that came the way of corporate India would have done little had it not been for the vision, risk taking abilities and entrepreneurship of some Indian promoters and companies. After years of inhibition and lack of self-belief, "alongside liberalization, one of the most exciting developments in India is private sector initiative."[1]

The corporate sector has been bullish riding on increased profits. The growth in net profit till December 2003 is reported to be 97.05 per cent. Given that the pace of growth was over ninety per cent in the previous year, the belief that the manufacturing sector could now be a growth driver has taken root.

With the government easing rules in terms of outbound investments including those for acquiring companies, Indian private sector firms confidently identified targets not just within the country but outside as well. According to Goldman Sachs, there were seventy-three cross-border mergersane acquisitions. Another observation by KPMG said of the total M&As involving Indian companies, forty-five per cent of the deal values were from the cross border route. The trend was clear that Indians were not bound to home turf and are ready to slowly move into the area of multinationals even if in a small way.

As a result, one found Reliance Industries outbidding other international bidders for US-based Flag Telecom. Bharat Forge went on to take hold of a German firm, Carl Dan Peddinghaus GmbH, and reports say that the Indian company is now the second largest forging company in the world. The Tatas have acquired Daewoo's truck division. VIP Industries Ltd acquired UK's Carlton International Plc, one of the leading luggage makers in the British world. Asian Paints picked up a Fiji firm, Azko Nobel's Taubman. The list is huge and this is just a short mention.

Companies like Videocon used the export market. Reports in the media suggest that Videocon had started dispatching television sets to the US market. The Tatas entered into an arrangement with MG Rover to sell the Indica as the City Rover. And in a different area, India's automobile components industry exported parts worth over US $ 1billion to markets such as the US and Europe.

---

[1] Goldman Sachs, India: Realizing BRICs Potential, April 2004.

Indian entrepreneurship was now there to be seen. What changed and how it happened was certainly a process that involved a mix of external as well as internal factors. Indians have learnt from the slump of the mid-1990s when over-capacity was created and exhausted only recently. Judiciousness has crept in and so has visions of growth and supremacy and this in a combined manner has created a more global mindset that does not necessarily ignore the domestic market.

The following chapter puts into perspective what Indian entrepreneurship is about. The setting is unusual — in an aircraft of a no-frills airline — an indication of Indian entrepreneurship and ingenuity. The chapter captures the mood of the Indian businessman through interviews with some of them and top executives of some of India's biggest corporate houses.

FROM LIBERALIZATION TO GLOBALIZATION

Govindraj Ethiraj

The loud drone of the Pratt & Whitney PW120 engines powering the two propellers on either side of the aircraft make casual conversation difficult. As does the constantly varying pitch in engine noise making you cast furtive glances outside the window to ensure that all is indeed well with this slightly ageing French ATR 42-320 turbo-prop aircraft.

The noise and the somewhat rudimentary flying conditions do not seem to dampen Captain G.R. Gopinath's enthusiasm, the man who manages the airline that owns this aircraft. He seems perfectly at home. The 'captain' is military, actually Gopinath does not fly at all, though he is, by any stretch, piloting a fairly daring aviation project — India's first no frills airline.

It is 6.30 in the morning and we are onboard an Air Deccan flight from Bangalore to Hubli, the airline's first route when it launched the first 'no-frills' service. Looking around, you realize this is clearly not what you would term a full flight, some fifteen seats are taken while this aircraft can carry forty-eight.

Earlier, standing in the airport lobby, clad in khaki chinos and his trademark light blue half-sleeve shirt with the Air Deccan logo emblazoned near his right picket, Gopinath strikes you as a quintessential entrepreneur as he works his hand-phone, battling what must be the vagaries of a start-up operation, conferring animatedly with colleagues in operations and people calling him for assistance in securing tickets.

Soon, we are climbing the little stairway and have scrambled for the best seats — no-frills means no seat reservations. A little after lift-off, as the aircraft strikes out in a north-westerly direction, we resume our conversation. Gopinath does not seem particularly concerned by the low occupancy, "It takes six months to build a sector like this," he says, adding with a laugh, "you should look at routes like Hyderabad-Bangalore, people are sitting on the wings!"

Gopinath has, as he takes pains to point out, been running a successful aircraft and helicopter charter service for the last ten years, most of the economic reforms period. Then, around two years ago, he decided to set up an airline. Which brings you to the first inevitable question of the day, why did he do that, plunge into a full-fledged airline, a business littered with carcasses of leased aircraft strewn across airports?

"People were calling me up and asking me to start an airline that connected smaller towns. That's how I decided to get into it," he says. But why now, you persist. Gopinath thinks, but not for too long. "Something's different today, there is a sense of optimism, of confidence, in India, by Indians, within India and outside. I just felt you could do it."

Gopinath says he was also influenced by India's software success story. Not to start his own IT company but to use cost-effective, Indian written software to build an ingenious, inexpensive, internet-based sales and ticketing network against, he points out, the advice of most consultants who suggested proven but expensive global packages.

A little over an hour later, having listened with interest to Gopinath's story and consuming a paid-for bottle of water and a sandwich (another no-frills facet) as the ATR descended swiftly into Hubli and thudded down on the runway, a thought was beginning to form in the head.

If India had formally embarked on a journey from liberalization to globalization, Air Deccan was one story that perhaps marked the end of that journey as it did, simultaneously, the beginning of a new Indian business order. An order governed by choice and not compulsion. An order that is not fazed by the countless hurdles and problems that still dot the Indian business landscape, rather where optimism and determination rule strong. This short story is about the order where the survivors of liberalization and the disciples of globalization, jointly represent the economic future of India.

Gopinath is of course, not the only example. There are countless more. Represented in businesses ranging from cellular phone companies to spanking new malls and multiplexes, from wineries to fitness centres, from management gurus and TV media moguls to small entrepreneurs and the IT and life sciences tigers of Bangalore, Hyderabad and Gurgaon, Indian businesses are increasingly united in achievement rather than the despair that so characteristically marked a businessman's outlook in the past decade.

Meet the globalised Indian entrepreneur, that batch of post liberalisation go-getters launching enterprises and businesses with an equal mixture of optimism and confidence and disdain for history or geography, a realization that for once, success will depend on their skills and abilities, not the dozen other reasons, ranging from government to god that brought businesses to their knees in the years past.

Seated in one of the many tastefully furnished, waterfront suites of the Taj Mahal Hotel in Mumbai, when asked recently whether he felt like a truly confident global entrepreneur despite sitting in Mumbai, Tata Group chairman Ratan N. Tata told this writer, "The environment enables one to do that. Do I feel I am playing that role with ease — No, we are starting down that road, I would humbly say that all these years I have been an Indian player and now, one is trying to be a citizen of the world." The Tata Group is a classic case of a clutch of Indian-owned companies, which have struggled hard with the fall-outs of liberalization — across scale, efficiency, technology and, most of all, internal attitudes — and can now claim to have traversed the distance to globalization, with some measure of success. Most Tata companies; Tata Steel, Tata Motors, Tata Consultancy Services and Indian Hotels (which owns the Taj Group) operate on some if not most global parameters.

Corporate India's attempts to globalize have been significantly bolstered by the truly globalised Indian brand to emerge from the 1990s that of IT. The IT brand marks the firm transition of Indian entrepreneurship through liberalization. It swept away, in one stroke, the traditional perceptions of Indian products and services as shoddy and backed by a largely incompetent workforce. Even the most anti free-market politician admits, "Thank God for that." Now, you may wonder why the reference to the IT sector has come up again. But this is relevant as it puts India's strides in the manufacturing sector into perspective.

A few hundred kilometers due east of Hubli, where Air Deccan now runs a daily service, and also in north central Karnataka, is the dusty and almost desolate Vijaynagar. Standing some fourteen storeys above the ground, atop the superstructure of a 'Corex' blast furnace and looking out at Jindal Vijaynagar's steel making facilities where there was once desolate land is Sajjan Jindal, the managing director and promoter.

The year 2004 should be when Jindal Vijaynagar could finally turn the corner. The company was born just after liberalization in 1991 and almost died in its throes, having taken on crippling, high cost debt and then faced with a long steel price slump. Both factors stand corrected for now, but what has also helped, in Jindal's words, is this. "Software has helped Brand India, it has helped our steel, it has helped companies like us." Jindal should know, his other company Jindal Iron & Steel, located closer to Mumbai, exports close to seventy per cent of its steel production, a difficult to imagine prospect even five years ago. Jindal. A quality boost has also helped, Jindal says its tough to make out the difference between Japanese and Korean steel on one hand, and Indian on the other. "The world knows we are capable of producing globally competitive products," he says.

Some five hundred kilometres south of Vijaynagar and about an hour's drive south-west of Bangalore is Bidadi, where another global Indian miracle has been nurtured. En route to Mysore, this clutch of factories is the Indian home to auto giant Toyota. While most visitors to Bangalore go back impressed with the Infosys campus, its youth-infused energy and acknowledge it as a temple of modern India, Bidadi is perhaps one of the many silent shrines to India's efforts to fight its way into manufacturing glory.

Toyota Kirloskar Auto Parts managing director Vikram Kirloskar's somewhat reclusive nature (akin to his Japanese collaborators) explains why Bidadi is known but not much talked about, except perhaps within manufacturing circles where even peers like the Pune-based Baba Kalyani light up in admiration. Kalyani incidentally runs Bharat Forge, another company that emerged from the trials and tribulations of liberalization to become a small but globally competitive ancillary maker.

The fact that Vikram's companies are not listed, helps — if listed Indian companies have adopted one global trait swiftly, it is the quarterly song and dance show that Wall Street and now Dalal Street thrive on. And yet, this show, when it rolls out on the trading floors of the New York Stock Exchange (NYSE) or at Nasdaq has played its own role in catapulting Indian companies to the global stage.

The Kirloskar group was a prominent manufacturing conglomerate until the 1980s, till liberalization happened and seemed to have almost swallowed the group. Vikram moved to Bangalore and started life anew with the Toyota joint ventures. "People change," he says, "when they see companies closing down around them. Even you yourself have to survive and change." Vikram's statement made on the shop floor of his modern plant, feeding Toyota worldwide with critical auto components made as he points out proudly, with Indian labour, aptly sums up Indian companies' struggle and the journey from liberalization to globalization.

This has been a journey where brutal restructuring and harsh corporate Darwinism have brought Indian businesses up, close and personal, with reality. One where the present is not taken for granted, leave alone the future, where the world is indeed a village and the wide-eyed optimism of the 1990s has given way to cautious but determined ambition.

But if the IT companies or the Kirloskars, Jindals and Bharat Forges are today facing up confidently to a globalised world today, having survived the turbulent 1990s and become lean and mean in the process, groups like Reliance with an unwavering determination to build scale have paced the Indian race to build truly global corporations.

Reliance, founded in 1966 by Dhirubhai Ambani, was one of the first groups to fight government mandated limits on manufacturing capacity, in hindsight perhaps the worst form of fetters any industrial enterprise anywhere could be bound with. And while most business houses were stumbling along a liberal licence regime in the 1990s gathering licences and permits and eventually investing in plants and operations, which would be bigger than before but still, largely uncompetitive in the global context, the Ambanis were powering ahead with truly global capacities, from investing Rs 9,000 crore to take up petrochemical capacity at one shot from 1.5 million tones to 6 million tones in 1997 to the 27 million tonne Jamnagar refinery, the world's largest grassroots refinery.

Realising where a firm's real competitive advantage lay, the Ambanis have also managed to match access to the biggest and the latest and then scoured the planet to fund it, at costs which were unheard of in the 1990s. Funds were raised at rates so fine even giant conglomerates across Asia, particularly in fast-growing Southeast Asia could only marvel. Reliance's 50 and 100-year bonds in 1997 were the first for any Asian company visiting the US debt markets, it was also the first

Indian company to raise funds through a Euro issue global depository receipt (GDR), in 1992.

Despite living in a reasonably tariff-friendly regime (rivals claim Reliance uses its clout in Delhi to keep it that way), Reliance was also one of the earliest to benchmark all its costs in dollars. "We are a dollar company, not a rupee company," then managing director and now vice-chairman Anil Ambani told this writer in the mid-1990s.

And yet, while Reliance became a globally competitive entity in India, it never really 'went' global. It used its scale and costs to make cheaper man-made fibre (compared to cotton) for the vast domestic market and thus fulfill one of many dreams of Dhirubhai, "to provide affordable clothing to Indians".

The same low-cost, best technology principle is being applied to mobile phones. Dhirubhai said he wanted to "make the tools of information technology and communication (infocomm) available to people at an affordable cost, they will overcome the handicaps of illiteracy and lack of mobility" and of course, he wanted a telephone call to be cheaper than a postcard. Interestingly, while a host of Indian companies have either exported successfully or even set up global operations overseas, only in the last year or so has Reliance begun talking geographically global. Recently, it bid for a petrochemical plant in Korea even as it announced the setting up of marketing outposts in countries like China. And as this book goes to press, Reliance Industries became the first Indian private sector company to record a net profit of over US $1 billion.

The journey from liberalization to globalization has thus, not necessarily involved the spreading of a global footprint, although many entrepreneurs and businessmen have confused the ability to export with being global. Indeed, many Indian businesses have gone overseas in previous decades, but more to escape the draconian business climate back home rather than build a cohesive global organisation or better still, a multinational company.

Not surprisingly, Indian business houses are now talking of an active 'global' strategy, inherently accepting that their international forays in the past were not a part of concerted globalised strategy. The Tata group is a good example. The group is now crafting a concerted global vision with a special team working on it, though it has had an international presence for decades, through several companies, including Tata Consultancy Services and Indian Hotels (The Taj Group).

In the last decade, many businessmen have worked tirelessly, turned adversity into opportunity, building globally competitive enterprises in India producing quality products. Global, not just in costs and operations but more importantly because free imports and alert, informed consumers have upped the local quality ante considerably. Indian companies have responded admirably to the challenges, of imports from outside and the general consumer yearning for quality within. The bogey of Chinese imports has remained largely that. Smart Indian companies like Mumbai headquartered Bajaj Electricals (another company which looked set to be gobbled up by liberalization) have actually built outsourcing channels into China, bringing in mass-made toasters, coffeemakers and steam irons and selling them under the Bajaj brand name.

Bajaj Electricals president and chief operating officer R. Ramakrishnan, for instance, is a regular visitor to the China's special economic zones in the Pearl River Delta, home to the world's largest collection of light engineering manufacturing facilities. This is where he ties up multi-million dollar outsourcing contracts in the same plants and even assembly lines that churn out appliances for some of the most quality-conscious markets in the world.

A fierce advocate of de-licensing for the small-scale industry in India, he believes India can still make it in this discipline of manufacturing but only if it is allowed to. Thus, while liberalization forced companies like Bajal Electricals to pull up their socks internally, globalization (in mind and on the ground) has allowed them to travel and seek opportunities elsewhere.

On the other hand, the two wheeler makers have proved capable of meeting and setting new quality and acceptance standards with customers, using their historical advantage of scale, albeit with some resistance initially, to their advantage. Not surprisingly, cheaper imports have not dented this market nor have foreign two-wheeler makers found the Indian market a walkover.

In Rahul Bajaj and B.M. Munjal, Indian industry has found businessmen who were perhaps a little on the defensive in the beginning but have today become silent votaries of truly global Indian corporations with all their manufacturing operations in India. Ditto with the Chennai-based TVS Group, who has stepped up its technology and innovation efforts after it broke off (somewhat acrimoniously it is believed) with Japanese two-wheeler giant Suzuki. The result: some of the world's most economically priced, quality two-wheelers, delivering value in efficiency, performance and design, giving Indian youth affordable (most Indian motorbikes sell in the 100 cc to 150 cc range) icons to be seen with. Check out the clearly well-to-do teenagers astride their bikes along Mumbai's posh, sea-side promenades on a Sunday evening or outside the hip, coffee shops of Bangalore and New Delhi and you will know what I am talking about.

If low power Indian bikes stand a chance of becoming truly global products, so do small, Indian cars. While Maruti leads the way in producing India's cheapest car with the 800, it is Ratan Tata's efforts and perhaps evangelizing with his dream small car project, the Indica, that has caused the automotive world to look at India as a possible small car sourcing nation for the world.

But a post-liberalisation, globally competitive market can be both good and bad news. In Pune's quiet and leafy Tata Management Training Centre campus with its colonial 'gymkhana' like central building, Harvard Business School professor Krishna Palepu gazes thoughtfully as he picks his words, "We need to realize that when India is in the spotlight, more people want to come and set up shop here. Which means the economy will be more competitive and people need to be prepared."

The harshest lesson here has perhaps been learnt by the two car companies, which had a stranglehold over the country's roads for four decades; Fiat (Premier Padmini) and Hindustan Motors. Car makers Hyundai, Ford, General Motors, Toyota and Honda have launched repeated onslaughts on the Indian market, not just decimating the incumbents but also giving each other a tough time, like they do in the rest of the world.

Similarly, in the consumer electronics and appliances businesses, from LG and Samsung to Whirlpool to Carrier, every global brand worth its name fights for shelf space across dealerships. Today, only a handful of Indian players, Mirc Electronics (maker of the Onida brand), Godrej, Videocon and BPL can be said to be fighting back.

Many Indian companies have handled liberalization admirably but are losing the battle of globalization. The reasons are many, one obviously being that Indian companies did not decide in time (or their egos held them back) what they could have done with themselves, that is, sell-out, merge or plain shut down. Another reason, as Harvard's Palepu says is: "The definition of a global company is that you can do business in a global environment. As India becomes a global economy, doing domestic business also requires a global mindset." Indian companies who do not or have not developed that global mindset are in serious trouble.

It may come as no surprise that foreign multinationals resident in India have not been spared this journey either. Older manufacturing companies like Siemens or pharmaceutical companies like Glaxo Smith Kline and Aventis have struggled equally, if not more, to clean up their domestic operations and come on par with their more competitive cousins in the region.

Both GSK and Aventis for instance have substantially revamped operations in the last few years by bringing in younger, Indian expatriate managers to restructure and change, down to the buildings and look and feel of the organizations. An hour's drive north of Mumbai in Siemens' switchgear plant at Kalwa, Siemens managing director J. Schubert proudly shows off his training centre where hundreds of employees learnt to work with new systems and processes.

If India Inc has somewhat successfully transited into globalization, are firms truly equipped to compete globally? Anecdotal evidence seems to suggest the answer is yes. Tata Steel's Jamshedpur plant is amongst the lowest cost steel producers in the world today and no company executive says they would want to move anywhere else. Sajjan Jindal is happy being in Vijaynagar (despite the fact that the sales tax concessions that once drew him there will go away some day) and hopes to go up to ten million tonnes (from around two million tonnes today) in the next few years and is confident his operations will run on global parameters.

Another true student of globalization is Suresh Krishna, managing director of Chennai-headquartered Sundram Fasteners, part of the TVS Group. Leaning back in his new corporate office located on the bustling Radhakrishnan Salai in downtown Chennai, Krishna says, "For the last twenty years, I have been telling my work-force that our destiny is not India, it is the world...and unless we become a truly global company...we cannot become a MNC...why should a MNC be an outside company?"

Krishna, who led the way in building a truly global, in this case, auto ancillary business (supplying radiator caps to General Motors), is also one of the few CEOs who is candid about the past. "My regret is that most of my life has been spent under the license raj. Our hands were tied but even under that regime if we managed to come up...I wish I was twenty years old." Then he adds, "Though I am still young, the future looks promising."

And promising it does, for the disciples of globalization, yearning to make a mark, be it in big industry or small, in services or manufacturing, in IT or media and fashion. And for consumers, who suffer from surfeit of choice not a lack of it, for youngsters and entrepreneurs, who will perhaps find opportunities in India greater and more fulfilling than those anywhere else.

On our Air Deccan flight back from Hubli, after a twenty-minute halt in Hubli, a young man walks up from behind the aircraft and congratulates Gopinath for starting this service. He hails from a family that runs a mid-size steel wire factory in Davangere, a few hours south of Hubli. And business has been tough with steel prices (an important raw material) playing truant. Yet, he is not complaining, least about what or how the government can make things better, a typical refrain with most business people.

"You are doing a great service to this part of the country," he tells Gopinath who reciprocates by saying these are precisely the customers he wishes to serve.

The young man and Gopinath strike a chord. "I returned from America because I wanted to do something in India. We heard and read so much about the changes, the prospects. We wanted a part of it." And he was not alone, he says. "All my batch mates from India decided we would return as soon as we finished our studies."

As the ATR begins its descent into Bangalore, Gopinath is catching a quick nap. He has a long day ahead of him, as do we and for thousands of software and BPO employees across the city, whose day began the previous night, it must have just ended. Indeed, for those who live in a globalised world, wherever they are, in Hosur or Gurgaon, there is no time to rest.

(*Many of the interviews here have appeared as part of the author's programmes on CNBC-TV18*)

TRADE

India's presence in international trade continues to be an embarrassing percentage point. This figure looks even worse, taking into account that the nation's population is about seventeen per cent of the world. But then there has been progress when the comparison is limited to the Indian economy. The contribution of trade as a percentage of GDP has more or less doubled from fifteen per cent in the early 1980s to over thirty per cent now.

Obviously, in the global scenario these figures mean little.

However, it is believed that the growth in IT and IT enabled services would contribute to higher values and an increased contribution to world trade. What is being pointed out is that India is slowly growing into a key off-shoring hub for many players in the manufacturing segment. The automobile sector (pointed out earlier) is one example where exports crossed US $1 billion. The textile sector is also expected to increase its penetration in the world market. And if farm sector reforms are implemented and show result, this segment would assume an important role in the global food market. Let us not forget that the government is continuing to pursue the setting up of special economic zones. While this has been an uphill task, there is an expectation that these zones would have some good news to offer in the near future.

Also, India is increasing its trade with neighbours such as China. This is significant since the two nations are the largest markets given the size of their populations. Besides, the geographical proximity reduces the landed cost of products. A greater dependence of the two nations could prove to be a significant development for world trade. According to reports in the media, the gross volume of foreign trade during January-June touched US $6.674 billion, a year-on-year increase of 93.1 per cent as against 39.1 per cent of Chinese trade volume in the same period. Significantly, India's exports to China were greater in value terms as against imports from the neighbouring nation.

While undoubtedly the future development of this relationship depends greatly on political will and India's association with nations such as the US, India is not expected to sleep over pursuing all kinds of tie-ups with countries in the Southeast Asian region. The recently concluded Indo-Thai Free Trade Agreement is one such example.

However, what has been key for India is not necessarily the percentage or the dollar value of trade but is that the swing is upward. According to reports, India's export growth touched over twenty per cent as the current financial year began. This is good news and should be seen in a positive light given the high growth levels last year and that the rupee is stronger than it was in the corresponding period.

But these growth levels have little relevance in the international market. What has been India's most noticeable achievement is its will and focus on trade matters. The trade talks at Cancun marked India's presence at the World Trade Organization (WTO) as never before. India's stance resulted in reports from the West claiming that the talks stalled because of this nation. And now, India and its allies have claimed victory after the Geneva round in July towed more or less the line that India had drawn in Cancun.

Certainly, the success in Geneva is something that will keep India smiling, it's the process and changed posturing over the years that has led to what India is in the trade scenario today.

What actually happened and how India evolved as a trade negotiator is put across in detail in the following essay.

THE SIGNIFICANCE OF CANCUN

Dr. Narendar Pani

Istory will record the WTO ministerial in Cancun in 2003 as a failure. No agreement was reached at the end of the ministerial. And whatever progress there was during the year, particularly in terms of making it easier for governments to overcome the barriers posed by patents while fighting epidemics, was made before the Cancun ministerial commenced. And yet from an Indian point of view, the ministerial is widely regarded as a turning point. Some of this favourable response can be discounted as being attributable to nothing more than the emergence of an articulate, legally trained negotiator in Arun Jaitley of the Bharatiya Janata Party (BJP) as the head of the Indian delegation. But it would be quite unfair, and inaccurate, to evaluate the entire Indian performance leading up to the Cancun ministerial entirely in terms of one personality or the other. The ministerial also marked the return of India as an important player in generating effective developing country alliances. The group of twenty-odd nations, including India and Brazil, marked the re-emergence of relatively better-off developing countries as a pole in international trade negotiations.

The significance of the emergence of this group in the run up to the Cancun ministerial can be fully appreciated only when seen in the context of the larger process of the evolution of the Indian negotiating position in the WTO. The debates within

India on the WTO — such as they are — tend to be preoccupied with immediate concerns. While attention to contemporary issues is inevitable, even desirable, they form only one part of the picture. The ability to respond to these and other issues also depends on the overall approach to trade negotiations, which typically evolves over a period of time. In order to understand why relating to contemporary issues is often so difficult, we need to explore the roots of traditional Indian positions. Even a casual look at these roots makes it obvious that no matter how weak some traditional positions may appear today, they had their relevance in the not too distant past. The challenge then is not just to overcome some mindless ideological barrier but to identify the specific economic rationales for India's negotiating positions that have now outlived their utility.

India's negotiating position at the WTO cannot be fully appreciated unless we remember that when the General Agreement on Tariffs and Trade (GATT) was signed in 1948, India was a poor developing country that had just gained Independence. India's negotiating position thus had all the scepticism of a poor country about the gains from free trade. There were enough economists influencing India's policy for the government to recognise the principle of comparative advantage. It was acknowledged that the overall benefit for all countries would be maximised if each one concentrated on doing what it did best. But Indian policy makers also knew that the distribution of this benefit was not even.

The developed nations, which had access to advanced technologies, got a lion's share of these benefits. There was also a growing consensus among developing countries, in the decades after Indian Independence, that world prices were shifting against primary products. And since primary products accounted for a significant share of the output of developing countries, this further distorted the share of these countries in the overall benefit from free trade. The Indian position was thus characterised by a certain scepticism about the benefits of trade. The scepticism wasn't so great as to prompt India to drop out of GATT as China did. But it encouraged it to take a minimalist view of trade negotiations. India led other developing countries in resisting any enlargement of the agenda. And it demanded that technology be transferred to the developing countries so that the benefits of free trade were shared more equally.

This overall developed-versus-developing-countries scenario should not lead us to believe that there was no common ground between the two groups of countries.

On the contrary, there were areas where the developed countries were themselves wary of the market. In some of these areas it suited India to cooperate, implicitly if not explicitly, with the developed world. This was particularly true when concerns about food dominated the policy agenda. Right until the Green Revolution in the late 1960s, India was a food deficit economy. There were in fact near-famine conditions in the mid-sixties. In that period, India was dependent on food aid from the developed countries. And the cost of that aid was reduced if the developed world subsidised their food production. A pre-Green Revolution India thus had reason to welcome food subsidies in the developed countries. The fact that this went against the demands of a free market only confirmed the overall scepticism about the benefits of free market economics.

The shared scepticism over free market economics between the developed and the developing countries was also not confined to areas of potential crisis like food. There were areas where the developed world's efforts to control markets provided huge growth opportunities for developing countries. The most striking example of a positive impact on the Indian economy of Western wariness over free markets was the case of textiles. The textile-importing developed countries were keen on fixing quotas for imports. By promising annual increments in the quotas they were able to convince developing countries like India to accept such a quota system. The system began with a one-year Short Term Agreement (STA) in the 1960s that dealt with cotton products. This was followed by a Long Term Agreement (LTA). And when the market for garments began to be dominated by non-cotton fibres, the Multifibre Arrangement (MFA) came into being. This system of quotas resulted in a phenomenal increase in India's garment exports. A growth that even the software export boom of the 1990s couldn't quite match.

India's trade negotiating strategy in the GATT years was thus one of, what may be called, pragmatic minimalism. It was minimalist in terms of limiting the areas that would be opened up to free trade. But the minimalism did not extend to preventing other interventions in international trade. By the late 1970s, the details of this approach had been worked out and a rhetoric settled upon. The consistent use of that rhetoric, in a way, made change appear unnecessary.

All the while, though, the basic characteristics of the Indian economy that prompted this strategy were not unchanging. The first premise of this strategy to take a beating was the assessment of India being a food deficit economy. The Green Revolution ensured that in terms of production, India would not remain a food deficit economy. If there still remained pockets of starvation it was not because physical stocks of food were not available. The challenge was more in terms of providing access to this food through increased purchasing power. As food aid receded into the past, India had little to gain from the food subsidies of the developed world. On the contrary, as unsold stocks of food grains mounted, India needed to find foreign markets for them. And the huge subsidies provided by the developed world to its farmers made it difficult for India to compete in those markets.

The conditions that helped India benefit from textile quotas were also changing, though not as dramatically. The impact of the quotas on garment exports was undoubtedly positive. It could not have been otherwise when readymade garment exports grew from a mere Rs 29 crore in 1970-71, three years before the coming of the Multifibre Arrangement, to Rs 25,478 crore in 2000-01. But as Indian garment exporters began to absorb the benefits of this boom, they began to wonder whether they could do even better without the restraints placed by quotas. This section of exporters began to point out that while garment exports were growing in absolute terms, India's share of the world market was not showing equally dramatic growth. And the share could not change dramatically as long as export quotas were being distributed. There was, thus, pressure built from at least one section of the exporters for India to demand a removal of all quotas in the world textile market.

Along with these sector specific changes, the overall scepticism about the benefits of trade was also coming under pressure. The inward-looking approach had had its impact on India's export performance. India's share of world exports had declined from around 2.5 per cent at the time of independence to around half a percent by 1975, and then stayed at that lower level.

The need to break out of this low export regime was recognised by the advocates of economic reform in the 1990s. At the same time, new Indian industries were making an impact in the world market. The communication revolution had put Indian software on the global stage. The export of software services soon became one of the fastest growing components of Indian exports. This growth in software exports took off even before Business Process Outsourcing (BPOs) became the subject of a global debate.

In responding to these changes, the official Indian negotiating position relied quite heavily on a developed-versus-developing-country approach. Where the changes in the Indian economy led to demands that fitted neatly into a conflict between developed and developing countries, it was quite quickly integrated into the Indian negotiating position. This was most evident in the case of textiles. There may have been some room for circumspection over whether the abolition of quotas would be an unqualified blessing. After all, such a free market would mean India would have to fight competition on price from poorer countries like Bangladesh, as well as competition on quality from others like China. But as far as India's trade negotiators were concerned, there were no such doubts about where the interests of India's garment exporters lay.

India pushed hard for an early removal of quotas. India protested against the developed countries' proposals to remove the bulk of the quotas only towards the end of the transition period. And the fact that this backloading of the removal of quotas became a part of the textile agreement of the Uruguay Round of GATT negotiations was generally presented as evidence of WTO agreements working against developing countries.

The changes in agriculture did not fit as easily into a simple conflict between developed and developing countries. If India was to find markets for its surplus agricultural produce, it needed to support the opening up of markets for agricultural products. This would have pushed India towards the Cairns group of agricultural countries, which included both developed and developing countries. But India's negotiators were not willing to abandon its traditional positions on food security. India's positions on agriculture thus tended to focus on the need to treat the developed and developing worlds differently. It wanted conditions to be imposed on the developed world but not on the developing countries.

The focus, almost exclusively, on the developing countries was reflected in the attitude to the WTO as well. In keeping with the traditional developing country perspective, there was scepticism about free trade. The WTO's efforts to promote trade were then seen as a scarcely disguised attempt by the developed world to gain control of global trade. Consequently, India was at the forefront of opposition to any effort to expand the WTO's agenda. The WTO may have been useful to the extent that a multilateral system was preferable to bilateral negotiations. But it had to be kept within limits. As the former Union commerce minister, Murasoli Maran, used to be fond of saying, the WTO was a necessary evil.

This minimalist approach to the WTO was, however, not the most efficient.

In order to minimise the role of the WTO, there was no attempt to link the lowering of trade barriers in India to global negotiations. Indeed, the lowering of tariff barriers, which was a part of the post-1991 liberalisation process, was done unilaterally. While this upheld Indian sovereignty, it was not the most efficient method of doing so. It meant that while India was lowering trade barriers substantially, it could not demand corresponding measures from other countries through trade negotiations. Thus, while India opened its markets, it could not use this process to prise open foreign markets for Indian products.

Within the realm of trade negotiations too, the minimalist approach had had its costs. With India only entering negotiations in new areas when it was clear that these could not be avoided, the country was not able to influence the early course the negotiations took. This could be expensive, as in the case of geographical indications. When an agreement on Trade Related Intellectual Property Rights within the Uruguay Round of GATT negotiations was first proposed, India was opposed to it. By the time it was clear that this agreement was inevitable, France had already managed to get the protection of geographical indications for Champagne. India later argued, quite rightly, that if Champagne could be protected on the grounds that it was the product of a specific geographical region, the same should hold for Basmati too. But not having played an active part in the negotiations when the ground rules were being defined, India has had to struggle to get even vague promises that the issue of geographical indications would be reviewed.

A minimalist approach to the WTO also makes it difficult to respond quickly enough to changes taking place in India's interaction with the global economy. For long, the main trade concern of India's software industry were the problems associated with Indians travelling abroad on work. The focus was thus on the so-called Mode 4 of the General Agreement on Trade in Services (GATS), which deals with the movement of natural persons. But with the dramatic growth of Business Process Outsourcing, the focus has shifted, at least partially, to the services provided from one country to another, the so-called Mode 1 of GATS. While identifying the new requirements are by themselves far from impossible, an approach that treats the WTO as no more than a necessary evil does not help in being fleet-footed when identifying the opportunities that the organisation offers to ward off such threats.

In terms of alliance building too, the traditional approach to developing countries had been coming under some strain. The Least Developed Countries (LDCs), at least since the 1990s, had been seeing their interests as being different from those of the better-off developing countries. Many of them were wooed with the promise of duty free access to the markets of the developed world. The possibility of a G-77 type of alliance covering all developing countries, including the least developed ones, thus receded. In continuing to seek such a broad alliance, India stood to lose the support of the relatively better-off developing countries without gaining the support of the LDCs. India thus stood the risk of being isolated, as indeed it was at the Doha ministerial. Murasoli Maran's holding out against all odds and even getting the ministerial extended may have won awards for bravery, but it did little for alliance building.

It is against this backdrop that India's position in the run up to the Cancun ministerial must be seen. India did continue to speak of building a developing country alliance, which all developing countries could join. But in the actual working of the alliance, the group of twenty-odd developing countries it helped put together had no Least Developed Country in it. India had, in effect, helped create an alliance of relatively better-off developing countries. And this alliance, with larger common interests, had a better chance of proving to be a stable influence in global trade negotiations.

The realism in alliance building was matched by an increasing flexibility on some other issues. India had developed a well-known rigidity on the four Singapore issues. It had refused to negotiate on these issues, namely, the relationship between trade and investment, the relationship between trade and competition, transparency in government procurement and trade facilitation. In the run up to the Cancun ministerial, there were some indications that India might be willing to step back from this rigid posture, particularly on the less sensitive of these issues, such as transparency in government procurement. This, in turn, sent out a clear message that India would not take a predetermined negative approach to negotiations, but would be willing to enter a process of give and take.

With the Cancun ministerial failing to reach an agreement, it is difficult to say just how far India would have gone down this path. Would it have actually given up its earlier position on some of the Singapore issues? Would it have been able to come up with an effective WTO based strategy to counter American protectionist moves on Business Process Outsourcing? We don't know.

But the run up to the ministerial provided sufficient indications that India may just be moving away from seeing the WTO as a necessary evil, to regarding it as a less-than-perfect but useful tool to help India regain a foothold in global markets.

THE ECONOMY

The Indian economy is possibly one of the toughest to fathom. The sheer size of the unorganized sector including the farm sector always makes it difficult to assume a close to accurate length, breadth and width of the economy. And with a huge parallel economy in existence, who knows how big the Indian economy is? There is speculation even amongst the most knowledgeable of economists that India has managed to keep inflation down despite low interest rates and a fiscal deficit of over five per cent of the GDP, since the parallel economy sustains the shocks. Even as inflation hovers close to eight per cent in August due to the continuing increase in global oil prices, some analysts believe that the level could have been higher. Who knows how true this is, but for sure the black side of the economy is a glaring reality that the government is still trying to get a hold of.

Most research-based economic papers including the ones from Goldman Sachs and the World Bank prefer not to delve too much into this issue and have focused on real numbers that relate to the organized part of India. According to a World Bank paper[1], "India's economic growth over the past two decades has been one of the world's fastest for large countries. In an outcome that few might have expected in the late 1970s, it jumped from

---

[1] India: Sustaining Reform, Reducing Poverty, World Bank.

an entrenched 3.5 per cent a year to close to 6 per cent during the 1980s and 1990s, substantially reducing poverty."

Morgan Stanley's Ruchir Sharma says that while India's progress is commendable, it is not a story of a revolution but of an evolution. "If one looks at it, India's steps have been erratic where 1991-92 saw a burst in reforms, 1995-96 consumers assuming a role and 2002 marked some progress in the area of privatization, power and telecom and this last year has been significant for different areas," he pointed out. True but Goldman Sachs[2] suggests that the process of reforms in India has been "at times, painfully slower than the likes of China, but it is occurring steadily nonetheless" and many feel that India has trudged along at a slow pace due to the democratic set up of the nation and coalition politics.

However, there is a political acceptance of the reforms process and the need to put the Indian economy on path to higher levels of growth. The Economist[3] states "the sign of economic good sense in India are increasingly robust...Perhaps the main reason for this is that, for the first time, there is now a broad acceptance of the desirability of economic reform." Corporate performance of the previous couple of years, as pointed in an earlier chapter, is an indication of digging into the benefits of economic reforms. Even the government, largely, keeping out of regulating the IT sector is being seen as one such measure, although in both cases the role of the individual cannot be discounted.

The expectations are huge. The GS paper says if "India could match China in the quality of its infrastructure and education, growth rates over the next five years could jump from an average of 6.1 per cent to 8.1 per cent." Mr Sharma feels that India is aiming low and has more to offer. "India should be aiming higher than just eight to nine per cent. The nation is starting

---

[2] Goldman Sachs Global Economic Paper 109, India: Realizing BRICs Potential.
[3] 'Let it Shine'; The Economist, February 21-27, 2004.

from a low base and there are many unproductive areas still to be tapped and economic performance has not necessarily been broad based barring this one good year. What will count, however, is whether the political class is up to it (pushing ahead with the reforms process)."

The optimism about India and its economy has a lot to do with the sustained growth levels in the corridor of six per cent for most of the past decade. What has excited interest more is the expectation that India is ready to invest more in infrastructure and education. The current government is talking about putting aside around two per cent of the GDP into education and pushing along with the road projects started by the earlier incumbent. If that is to happen, the growth prospects are huge particularly given the general openness that already exists. Economists are also pretty optimistic claiming that the growth levels in China had a lot to infrastructure building and now it seems India is slowly going down the same path.

India's economic performance in 2003-04 has been stupendous by any standard. With the GDP touching 10.4 per cent for the third quarter, ridding on a good monsoon and an improving manufacturing sector performance, it is being estimated that the Indian economy grew at 8.2 per cent. What seems to attract people is the future potential arising from a very young population that could adapt to things more quickly. Points out Farokh Balsara, a partner at Ernst & Young in India, "No other nation is so young — seventy per cent of the population is in the age bracket of thirty-five years. This means that future businesses run on new technology would be easily managed and absorbed by the younger population."

It is apparent that the optimism about the Indian economy comes from the realization that the nation that is said to "have been 'emerging' for years, has at last come out."[4] Even if the projections about India may turn out to be a bit over-stated, the

---

[4] 'India's shining hopes', The Economist, February 21-27, 2004.

broad basing of the economic process is on the cards and the expectation is that this would mean increased productivity and higher growth levels. The current Congress-led government known as the United Progressive Alliance is expected to address key issues such as agricultural reforms, increased expense on education besides pushing ahead with policies that encourage investments. While implementation is the key to such policy initiatives, the path seems to be more in line with global suggestions that India needs to address issues such as farm sector reforms, education and poverty.

The following chapter goes deep into the politics of the Indian reform's process and the performance of the Indian economy. This puts into perspective 2003-04 and the new face of the Indian economy. Significantly, the chapter suggests that the reform process actually took off two decades ago and not in 1991 that marked the opening up of the Indian economy.

REFORMS, GETTING IT POLITICALLY CORRECT

Abheek Barman

The volume of writing on India's post-1990 reform programme over the last decade will fill several bookshelves. Supplemented by industry surveys, sector summaries, analysts' reports on companies, industries and sectors there is enough material, much of consistently high quality, to make for a respectable library. One aspect that is consistently under-reported and receives scant attention in this voluminous bibliography is the political process underlying reform. By bringing these aspects into focus, the economic performance of the past year or so becomes greater, if not significant, given the way Indian policies evolved and faced the stress of domestic differences and external factors.

This article focuses on the interplay of politics, individuals and events that triggered the Rao-Singh reforms of 1991-96. The role of the Gulf war in triggering the crisis is highlighted, since a lot of the literature glosses over this subject. I also believe that India's reforms actually began in 1984, a view that is gradually gaining ground now. We conclude with a tentative forecast of the broad policy imperatives of the government elected in the 2004 general elections.

Sriperumbudur, 1991

The campaign for the general — Lok Sabha — election of 1991 stretched through the hot summer months of May and June. Around ten in the evening, Rajiv Gandhi, leader of the out-of-power Congress party, arrived in Sriperumbudur, a sleepy town in the southern state of Tamil Nadu.

As he made his way towards a makeshift stage through a huge crowd, a bespectacled girl called Dhanu, carrying a sandalwood garland, stepped close. Anushya, a policewoman, tried to move her away but Rajiv said, "Let everybody have a chance," and allowed Dhanu to garland him. She stooped to touch his feet, Rajiv bent to help her up, and Dhanu pressed a switch that exploded a bomb strapped to a vest she was wearing. The blast killed Rajiv, his assassin and many others nearby.

Eighteen hours after Rajiv's assassination, the Congress' highest group, the Working Committee, met to condole his death — and decide on a new leader. Five people, Maharashtra's Sharad Pawar, Madhavrao Scindia and Arjun Singh from Madhya Pradesh, Rajasthan's Rajesh Pilot and UP's N.D. Tiwari fancied their chances of heading India's oldest party.

Ex-finance minister Pranab Mukherjee, who had tried to hurriedly project himself as prime minister after Indira Gandhi's assassination in 1984, wisely kept out of the scramble this time and insisted on inviting Rajiv's grieving widow Sonia Gandhi to head the party. At the end of a 100-hour meeting, during which the leader's place was kept vacant and no tea or coffee was served, Mukherjee recorded Sonia's refusal to head the Congress and proposed the name of septuagenarian P.V. Narasimha Rao, who had retired from politics before the elections, to head the party. Nobody saw him as a threat, everybody was relieved that none of the other contenders would get the top job in the party, so Rao came out of retirement to head the Congress.

New Delhi, 1991

When the election results were declared, it was found that the Congress had won 232 seats, many more than what it had been projected to win. Opinion polls after the first phase of elections — before Rajiv's killing — had pegged the final Congress tally between 180-190 seats. Clearly, the assassination at Sriperumbudur had swung votes for the party. Still short of the 272 seats required for majority, Congress was comfortably placed to form the government with the support of small parties. Thus Narasimha Rao, written off by everybody within Congress and almost forgotten by the rest of the country, became India's prime minister on June 21, 1991. The popular view of India's economic reforms programme begins at this moment, with Narasimha Rao taking office at the head of a Congress government, following two years of chaotic governance by the National Front, a coalition headed by ex-Congressman V. P. Singh.

Singh had toppled Rajiv's Congress from power in elections held in 1989. His coalition, formed with the sole goal of keeping the Congress out of power, lacked any cohesive structure. He had to lean on the Left, and incongruously on the Hindu-revanchist Bharatiya Janata Party as well, for support to keep his regime going. Unsurprisingly, the government fell when the BJP launched a vicious campaign to polarize India along religious lines through late-1989 and 1990. With the help of people from the imploding National Front, Chandrashekhar, a wily political manipulator with only fifty-seven MPs with him, made a bid for power. With the support of the Congress, he formed a government that lasted six months, after which Rajiv pulled the plug and called for elections.

Meanwhile, India's economy was in trouble. Five years of high growth, driven by piecemeal deregulation during the Congress regime of 1984-89, had overheated a still largely closed economy. Overseas borrowings had soared and inflation was high. If the currency were on a float, the rupee would have depreciated sharply against other currencies, slowing down imports and boosting export earnings, but India's fixed exchange rate regime didn't allow for that.

Then came the final blow: the Gulf War, when America and its allies attacked Iraq after the latter's invasion of Kuwait. India's tottering economy went into free fall. The Gulf War was a defining moment for India's policymakers, yet the effect it had on precipitating the crisis and triggering the wave of reform that followed has never been analysed in the flood of literature that India's reforms have spawned.

Iraq, 1990

By 1989-90, India was importing about twenty-six million tonnes of crude and refined oil — about half its total requirement. More than seenty-five per cent of these imports were through bilateral agreements. The rest was purchased spot from global markets. Official figures show that the share of Iraq in oil imports then was less than ten per cent of total imports, but doesn't show us the real degree of India's contemporary reliance on Iraqi oil.

That's because another eighteen per cent or so of India's total oil imports came from the Soviet Union. Most of the Soviet oil was actually from Iraq, obtained through a mutually beneficial triangular relationship between Iraq, the Soviets and India: Baghdad supplied oil to Moscow in return for guns and machinery. The Soviets sold oil to India for rupees according to a rupee-ruble barter trade arrangement. This helped Delhi, which had a chronic shortage of foreign exchange, to fund purchases of fuel and other imports.

On the eve of the Gulf War, which was triggered by Iraq's August 2, 1990 invasion of Kuwait, India had huge construction and engineering projects in Iraq.

Though interrupted by the 1980-87 war between Iran and Iraq, in the three-year period from 1986-88, more than thirty-three per cent of the total foreign projects awarded to Indian companies were signed off from Baghdad. By 1991, it is reckoned that Baghdad owed US $965 million to 26 Indian companies.

After the end of the Iran-Iraq war, Delhi's exports to Baghdad jumped from Rs 180 million in 1987-88 to Rs 1.3 billion in 1989-90, more than double the 1980 figure of Rs 520 million.

More trade and investment inevitably meant that the number of Indians living and working in Iraq and Kuwait would go up sharply. It did: the number of expatriates in these two countries jumped from 1,250 in Kuwait and 650 in Iraq in 1984, to more than 180,000 on the eve of the Gulf War. These numbers came from a letter written by V.P. Singh to Parliament in September 1990. These expatriates sent back a large share of their income as foreign exchange remittances to India, which contributed a large share as 'invisibles' to current account earnings.

Of course, politics had a large role to play in determining these relations. Successive Congress governments since the first one led by Nehru, supported the Arab cause in the Arab-Israel conflict. Since the late 1950s, when Iraq's last monarchy led by King Faisal II was overthrown, the Ba'ath regime backed India during occasional rivalries with Pakistan. Given that, support to Iraq was an important chip that Indian politicians used to woo Muslim votes. Though V.P. Singh's National Front government was backed by the Hindu-majoritarian BJP from the outside, Singh recognized the importance of Muslim support for his party and was compelled to take Iraq's side through the protracted diplomatic pow-wows before the attack on Iraq.

Before the Gulf War began, India moved to substitute for the expected loss of Iraq crude. It negotiated imports from suppliers in Saudi Arabia, Dubai, Qatar and UAE. But costs soared: from an average of $16 per barrel in June, to US $24 per barrel in August and to US $32 per barrel by October. The import bill for fuel, around Rs 5 billion per month during June, July and August 1990, shot up to an average of Rs12.2 billion per month during the following six months.

The finance ministry's Economic Survey for 1991-92 gives a breakup of the financial implications of the Gulf War. These include the direct impact of the Gulf crisis on the balance of payments, worth about US $2.9 billion, of which US $2 billion was from additional petroleum import bill, US $280 million due to the fall in export earnings from West Asia (of which US $150 million was from Iraq and Kuwait) and US $114 million worth of dues from Iraq that had to be written off or 'deferred.'

As Indians left the Gulf in hordes, Delhi also had to reckon with a loss of US $273 million worth of incomes that wouldn't be sent back, and the US $200 million bill for getting Indians out of the Gulf in a hurry. To do that, the government organized the largest civilian airlift in history, ferrying more than 100,000 people back home. The Economic Survey added a terse footnote to this roll call of financial disaster, noting that apart from these direct costs, there was a rise in interest rates and a sharp drop in tourist arrivals.

The Reformers

Manmohan Singh was supposed to go to a friend's house for lunch on June 21 — the day Rao took charge of the new government. In the event, his wife Gursharan, had to call their hosts and cancel the evening's plans: Singh had been called by the prime minister around eight in the morning and asked to take charge of India's finances not as an advisor or a guide but as the finance minister. Singh was an economist trained at Cambridge and Oxford but had quit academics to become a technocrat. He had advised ministries, run the Reserve Bank of India, headed the Left-leaning South Commission at Geneva and held the top job at the University Grants Commission — the hub of India's state-run university funding system — when Rao called him.

To assist him, Rao appointed Palaniappan Chidambaram, a Harvard-trained lawyer-politician with liberal economic ideas as commerce minister. Singh would handle the big-picture stuff — exchange and interest rate liberalization, banking and financial reforms and so on; Chidambaram would handle the nitty-gritty of trade liberalization. Rao himself would provide the political air cover as the team went about its job. Rao himself was not an instinctive economic liberaliser: he'd been quite at home in Indira Gandhi's Left-leaning regimes that, through the late 1960s to the late-'70s, tightened the noose of controls around the economy's neck.

But he was a pragmatic politician, one who realized that the old order was floundering and something new had to be tried to save India from going under. And to his eternal credit, he was willing to fire the first shot announcing the changes to come.

Following colonial practice, India's budgets were presented after five in the evening. The July morning of the day when Manmohan Singh was supposed to present his first budget, journalists landed up at the office of the industry ministry, expecting nothing but the usual dreary press releases about performance of state-owned enterprises. Over the next hour or so, they couldn't believe their ears. As industry minister, Narasimha Rao announced that over eighty per cent industries were to go off licensing immediately. Restrictive anti-monopoly laws that actually squeezed the ability of companies to grow were relaxed.

As Rao droned on in his pedantic way about how everything he was doing was in the spirit of continuity, it became clear that it was anything but. Here was a radical break from the past. In the evening's budget, Manmohan Singh unveiled the rest of the reforms package.

The breakneck pace of reform lasted about two years. By then, Manmohan Singh's budgets had become, annual celebration an of policy drama — eagerly awaited, closely watched, interpreted threadbare. By the yardsticks of the first two years, the 1993-94 budget looked wan. By 1994-95, Manmohan Singh's penultimate budget, it was clear that the pace of reform was flagging. For two years, producers' (or wholesale price index) inflation had shot over ten per cent, the government's main priority was to bring prices to heel. Rao was keenly aware that high prices could topple governments in polls, elections were due in 1996 and his instruction to the Central bank, the RBI was clear: bring inflation to heel.

THE REFORM YEARS

1991-92

- ☐ Rupee is devalued by 18 per cent
- ☐ Import licencing is scrapped for many things
- ☐ About 80 per cent of industries delicensed, number of licensed sectors shrinks from about 100 to 18
- ☐ Disinvestment starts, mops up Rs 3,000 crore
- ☐ Sharp 15 per cent cut in deficit planned
- ☐ Fertiliser price hikes to reduce sops
- ☐ 51 per cent FDI allowed in important sectors
- ☐ Liberalization of import system

1992-93

- ☐ Income tax rates and number of slabs dropped
- ☐ Wealth tax abolished on productive assets
- ☐ Excise shifted from specific duty to ad-valorem
- ☐ Many import curbs lifted
- ☐ New exchange rate management system in place
- ☐ Customs duties cut
- ☐ Peak tariffs down to 110 per cent
- ☐ FERA relaxed
- ☐ ONGC corporatised, government cuts stake in Maruti Udyog Ltd from 60 per cent to 50 per
- ☐ Private sector enters value-added telecom and oil refining, private equity in roads
- ☐ FIIs allowed into private companies

1993-94

- ☐ Excise slabs merged
- ☐ Capital gains tax on FIIs cut
- ☐ Dual exchange rates merged
- ☐ Cars and white goods delicensed

- ❑ Large-scale garment making allowed FDI
- ❑ SBI enters IPO market
- ❑ Interest rate floors brought down
- ❑ Disinvestment flops

1994-95

- ❑ Bulk drugs delicensed, 51% FDI allowed
- ❑ Disinvestment raises nearly Rs 5,000 crore
- ❑ Private players in telecom: First cellular services in metros
- ❑ Telecom bids attract Rs 100,000 crore, run into trouble
- ❑ Enron enters Maharashtra
- ❑ Private bids for roads, tolling allowed
- ❑ First private airlines: Jet, EastWest, Damania start
- ❑ Takeover code passed

1995-96

- ❑ First foreign car-maker, Daewoo, makes Cielo
- ❑ Telecom regulator Trai legislated
- ❑ Kelkar draws up 7-year oil deregulation plan
- ❑ Disinvestment flops
- ❑ SBI lists overseas
- ❑ Primary dealerships begin operation

1996-97

- ❑ Import duties cut
- ❑ 48 industries can get 51 per cent FDI through the automatic route
- ❑ Consumer electronics de-licensed
- ❑ Disinvestment Commission set up
- ❑ FIIs allowed to invest in unlisted companies
- ❑ Overseas borrowing made easier

1997-98

- ❏ Income tax slashed from 40 per cent to 30 per cent
- ❏ Corporate tax rate cut
- ❏ Dividend tax on individuals gone
- ❏ Tax breaks for telecom, power and oil exploration
- ❏ NRIs can invest 100 per cent in priority sectors
- ❏ Telecom licenses become tradable
- ❏ Electricity regulators — CERC and SERC — legislated
- ❏ Tata — SIA airline joint venture disallowed due to the bar on foreign airlines investing in domestic carriers

1999-00

- ❏ IT import duties slashed
- ❏ Simplified tax regime
- ❏ Free import for 340 items
- ❏ Government 'downsizing' mentioned for the first time
- ❏ 100 per cent automatic FDI for power, roads, bridges, ports
- ❏ Pre-payment of ECBs allowed
- ❏ Rediff, Sify do ADRs

2000-01

- ❏ Customs duty goes up
- ❏ Quantitative regime ends, 1400 remaining items freed
- ❏ Defense spending up
- ❏ Banks allowed to enter insurance
- ❏ Insurance regulator, IRDA sets out norms for private players, 11 players get insurance licenses
- ❏ Maruti to be privatized

2001-02

- ❏ Disinvestment department gets a minister
- ❏ Balco, VSNL, IPCL, hotels go on block

- ❑ Highway development project renamed Golden Quadrilateral

2002-03

- ❑ Proposal to reform indirect taxes and shift to VAT
- ❑ Row breaks out over decision to sell BPCL, HPCL, sell offs stalled by Supreme Court
- ❑ Power distribution privatized in New Delhi
- ❑ 20-year plan to link rivers proposed

2003-04

- ❑ Excise cuts drop prices on items like cars and air-conditioners
- ❑ Customs rate drops, special additional duty is abolished
- ❑ Unified license introduced, ends dispute between cellular and WLL mobile service providers
- ❑ Reliance, ONGC and Cairns make big oil and gas discoveries
- ❑ PSU equity sales net Rs 15,000 crore, privatization is off, selective sale in the markets is in

The bank, then headed by Chakravarthy Rangarajan, applied monetary brakes and inflation dropped dramatically. Rangarajan, heavily influenced by rational expectations theory, which held that monetary policy couldn't influence output in the short term, but could change long-term inflationary expectations — continued with the tight money policy for almost a decade. In the process, India's long-term trend inflation rate fell from eight per cent through the 1970s to the early '90s, to about five per cent in the subsequent ten years.

Not everyone was happy — finance worried about the contractionary effect of tight money on the economy, businesses fretted about how they would fund investments as interest rates went north.

Slowdown and Defeat, 1996

Neither reform, nor tight money could save the Rao government from defeat in the 1996 elections. Though an enormous amount of work had been done to unshackle the economy from controls, reform couldn't turn into an election winner. Two powerful new trends had risen on India's political landscape. One was fragmentation of the polity as small parties focused on regional and local issues came to power in states. Two, the divisive politics of caste and religion that been simmering since the early 1990s were scooping votes away from the Congress.

Within the Congress, Rao, a cunning but un-charismatic politician, created a lot of problems. Rao knew he was surrounded by ambitious leaders raring to take his job away, so his response was to set satraps against each other. As his government, rather ineffectually, probed a stock exchange scam in 1994, they came across papers that suggested Chidambaram's wife held stocks in some companies that were being probed. Though there was nothing illegal or underhand about this, media feasted on the story and Chidambaram offered to quit, expecting his prime minister to back him and turn down the resignation. To his shock, Rao calmly accepted the letter, an action that not only cost Chidambaram his ministry, but also implied that the PM didn't trust the integrity of one of his closest lieutenants. Before the 1996 elections, Chidambaram would quit the Congress and join Tamil leader Moopanar in the new Tamil Maanila Congress.

People like Manmohan Singh believe that Rao lost his nerve to reform after one of the most decisive days in modern India's history — December 6, 1992 — the day fundamentalists of the RSS-BJP-Shiv Sena-Bajrang Dal combine destroyed a 500-year-old mosque in the town of Ayodhya in Uttar Pradesh. The BJP state government of Kalyan Singh, naturally, did nothing to stop the demolition. The jury is still out on why Narasimha Rao, who certainly had intelligence that something drastic could happen in the tinderbox atmosphere of Ayodhya, did nothing to stop the demolition.

When Did the Reforms Really Begin?

Despite the mutterings of naysayers and prophets of doom, reforms survived the Rao regime. This is less surprising than it seems. Of course, the Rao-Singh reforms were driven by the urgency of having to comply with the International Monetary Fund (IMF) workout after India received a substantial loan package to tide over the crisis of 1990. But actually, reforms had begun a good six years earlier, during the regime of Rajiv Gandhi. Economist Arvind Virmani has long pointed out that India's real growth surge began in the mid-1980s, driven by Rajiv's reforms and that the effect of these initial measures on long-term growth was actually more profound than anything before. It is useful to recall what happened then.

The Rajiv regime seized upon some half-hearted liberalizing begun in the last days of his mother, Indira's, time. His administration encouraged capital imports and commodity exports, some industrial deregulation, and tried to rationalize the tax system in a modest way. In the first year, it eliminated curbs on imports of machinery, and cut tariffs on imported capital goods by sixty per cent. Taxes on profits from exports were halved, the number of industries subject to licensing was brought down from seventy-seven to twenty-seven in 1988. In its last days, the government began to end price controls on industrial materials like cement and aluminum.

Berkeley economist Brad DeLong writes: "The consequence of this first wave of economic reform was an economic boom. Real GDP growth averaged 5.6 per cent per year over the Rajiv Gandhi administration, while real rupee exports grew at 15 per cent per year. The country's net capital import bill rose to 3 per cent of GDP by the end of the 1980s. This growing foreign indebtedness — more than a quarter of exports were going to pay international debt service by the end of the 1980s — set the stage for the exchange crisis of 1991."

Was the crisis avoidable?

Should India have borrowed less?

DeLong argues: "It is hard to argue that India would have been better off in the 1980s had it not borrowed from abroad. (It is easy to argue that it would have been better off had it followed a more realistic exchange rate policy in 1989 and 1990.) With limited exports, foreign borrowing is an extremely valuable way to finance capital goods imports. If...capital goods imports are extraordinarily productive sources of technology transfer, then even extreme vulnerability to international financial crises as a result of foreign borrowing is a cost that weighs lightly in the balance relative to the benefits of one's firms being able to buy more foreign-made capital on the world market." What could have saved India from crisis, he points out, is a flexible exchange-rate policy that would have minimized the risk of a run on the rupee.

By incorporating the Rajiv years in the reform calendar, it is easier to see what gives Indian reforms the depth they have: a twenty rather than thirteen-year history, with concomitant institutional depth.

Thus, as finance minister of the Left-supported United Front (UF) coalition government, Chidambaram — a friend and colleague of Rajiv Gandhi — presented the 'dream budget' of 1997-98. Critics of the UF regime point out that it pushed through wage hikes for Central government employees by triggering the Fifth Pay Commission's recommendations. This provoked demands from employees of state governments for higher pay. Government spending on wages went up dramatically and created fiscal trouble in many cash-strapped states. While this is undeniable, it should also be remembered that India's very high GDP growth rates during the years 1996-97 and 1997-98 were a direct result of the wage hike, which bolstered the GDP numbers.

What Now?

From 1998 to 2004, two successive coalitions led by the BJP have held power. While in Opposition, the party was strongly protectionist and arguing for swadeshi — a form of autarkic, India-can-do-it-on-its-own brand of economics. It opposed private entry into insurance when Chidambaram first brought up the issue in Parliament. Its first policy statement in power — Yashwant Sinha's first budget, seemed to confirm everyone's worst fears. "India shall be built by Indians," he thundered. Yet, over the years, as the BJP came to terms with the realities of policymaking in an increasingly globalising world, its economic policy became indistinguishable from that of any other reformist regime.

Through April-May 2004, India saw one of its most protracted — and dramatic — political contests in its history: the Lok Sabha elections. The results are well known, the Congress is back in power after eight years, not alone but supported by allies including Left parties with sixty-two seats, which is its highest tally ever. The new government has published a Common Minimum Programme (CMP) — a manifesto for the coalition — that has provoked reactions ranging from alarm to admiration. In many ways, what's happening today has startling parallels events of the first seen years of reform.

Like 1990-91, the entire Gulf region, indeed the Arab world, is rocked by crisis with its epicenter in Iraq. Manmohan Singh is back in government, this time as prime minister. Chidambaram is back at North Block, home of the finance ministry.

America's occupation of Iraq has run into trouble, instead of a smooth handover of power to the Iraqi people and the beginnings of a democratic government in the heart of the Middle East, the whole country is slipping into civil war. Oil prices have hardened — at the time of writing, benchmark Brent and Texas crude had crossed US $40 per barrel levels touching almost US$ fifty per barrel. American retail fuel prices have jumped 50 per cent in five months. India's state-controlled oil retail sector has so far held prices at reasonable levels, but this might prove unsustainable.

India's equity markets are volatile, buffeted by investor jitters about Asian markets following Beijing's moves to cool down an overheating economy and fears of bad debt in Chinese banks. Investors are yet to make up their minds about what to make of the new government's policies — is India taking a sharp, Left-of-Centre turn? Will this mean reforms will be abandoned? Is the country headed for a crisis?

It is almost certain that reforms will continue; but with some change as the government's priorities shift towards increased public investment in areas like irrigation, rural credit, healthcare, education and so on. Finding funds for these projects — a proposal to hike education spend to six per cent of GDP from the current four per cent will cost an extra Rs 5,000 billion — will be a challenge, but it is impossible to argue against the desirability of these reforms. Or to ignore the fact that these are sectors that have been bypassed by policy over the last six years.

But economic reform has worked in every sector where it has been attempted: India in 2004 is vastly different from what it was in 1991 or 1984. Foreign exchange reserves, down to US $1.1 billion — worth a fortnight's imports — in 1990, are now a healthy US $119 billion, leading bankers to forecast an appreciation of the rupee particularly when oil prices stabilize. India's IT and IT enabled services are growing fast. Its share of the US $120 billion business process outsourcing market is still a small US $2 billion. In three years, this could grow to five times its current size. Mobile telecommunication, unheard of in 1991, now has more than thirty-five million users, with the number of subscribers doubling each year in the last four years.

If we take the reform countdown back twenty years, we see a parallel movement in the polity — decentralization, increased powers for state governments, local bodies, village *panchayats* (local self government). Rajiv Gandhi pioneered the *panchayati raj* (rule of the local self government) movement, taking lessons from states like Kerala and West Bengal, where local governments are active. The key to better delivery of public investment and more efficient use of resources is decentralization.

The rise of regional, or caste based, or linguistic parties through the 1990s showed that voters were unhappy about the failure of large parties to deliver results. The rise of coalition politics has helped push greater powers for states and local government. These are all gains, a silent revolution paralleling the achievements of the economic reforms.

They are also measures to transform the world's largest democracy into one of the most prosperous economies in the world as well.

INDIA IN PRINT

Not undermining any other source of information, it is a fact that had the media not stepped in to carry reports on India, the story would have been left with just a few — and possible a story untold to those who were not the protagonists. The media's role has been significant in creating a sentiment, pride, besides throwing up a debate on what India stands for and whether it has the ability to sustain relatively high levels of growth and emerge as a super economic power in the years to come.

We cannot ignore its hard driving role that worked both as an under current spicing the Indian flavour and that of a storyteller.

READING THE LARGE PRINT

For over six months, starting somewhere in the month of October 2003, the Indian mainline media — mainly the urban English media — repeatedly told its readers that India was on a high and there was every reason to 'feel good'.

Don't look back at miserable 2002-03 or the several droughts that hit the southern states of Karnataka and Andhra Pradesh over the previous few years, or the Gujarat riots — that's history. India is on its way to being an economic superpower in a couple of decades. We are not saying it, global investment firms are saying it and a majority of the mainline press reiterated in its reports.

True, this was and is a well-received economic analysis of Goldman Sachs. But what was hardly highlighted was the fact that India had issues on hand that of structural changes and education, the economic paper of GS[1] had pointed out. Even a World Bank report that expected high growth levels of India suggested that the economy had hurdles in low literacy levels, the education system and poverty. But this was the fine print, not fine enough to keep the readers feeling good.

There seemed to be a concerted effort to focus only on positives and how the urban media defined reforms with a possible objective of creating an aura around the successes of Indians and India at large. While this was as good as the best

---

[1] Goldman Sachs, Global Economics Paper No 99, Dreaming With BRICs: Path to 2050.

of public relations campaigns that India had experienced, the endorsement of the media made sure that the huge readership base of Indians were being sold a 'credible' story that had little of any other side to it.

This then could explain why (barring a few instances) that certain small print facts of reports by Goldman Sachs and other entities were not projected as it could have ruined the party for the media that seemed to have insulated itself from harsh realities and was catering only to a limited market. However, even as this may have been part of an agenda or a collusion of agendas, or mere self-censorship and self-interest, this form of reporting did have its own bit of significance.

Urban India was lapping it up and a certain sense of pride did creep into the psyche of those who picked up these papers. This was not bad at all as Indians did need to pump their chests and feel good for the progress that many of their clan was making. After all, India was 'shining'. Even a television programme asked the people present in the studio whether India was progressive and shining, and the majority did tilt in favour of the affirmative. In fact, one of the participants said that he could see it all around and for him not waiting for a telephone connection was his way of gauging progress and connecting with the media's hype.

The approach of the media also put pressure on the government to shift some focus to economics rather than only politics. This could be one of the reasons why the elections of 2004 had the economy as one of the key planks. It is a different matter that the ruling coalition lost the elections, the reason in this case was attributed to the over use of an advertising campaign that attempted to take credit for every economic achievement.

Maybe such coverage of the media did contribute to a sentiment that may have created an atmosphere for increased self-belief and confidence. Just maybe, as an analyst pointed out cautiously, indicating that such a conclusion had not yet been established by any specific measuring system. But he admitted that the media did have a strong influence on the impressionable Indian mind.

So then this form of reportage was expected to work particularly when the Indian psyche is so deprived of praise and achievements that acknowledgements from any quarter is welcomed. And when the West says it, well, it is difficult to bring an Indian down from the heights of jubilation. Typically, points out a social scientist, such 'highs' leads to positive thinking and often translates into celebrations that include some form of consumption and that's good for the industry!

Aha! So was this the agenda behind the media hype?

Could be. Still, one can't snatch the truth away that the news reports were not untrue, they may just have been a bit too in-the-face or overstated that could have been a result of being starved of positives in the Indian scenario and the monotony of the typical poverty, corruption, tangled legal system and coalition politics reporting had tired and bored the Fourth Estate. (It could also have been part of an agenda, as stated earlier in this write up.)

An example of going over the top is the reaction to an international news report suggesting that India's retail mall hub, Gurgaon, could be the Asian retail capital. It set off a "round of self-congratulatory stories on this subject within the Indian media. The kids eating at McDonalds. The 'mushrooming' of fast food joints. The idea of whole families spending much of their weekend at the Malls".[2]

On another instance, the papers of December 21, 2003 screamed out that India had foreign exchange reserves of over US $100 billion. "Never before has dry economic news been celebrated so widely in India," remarked Kaushik Basu in an article on the Indian economy.[3]

---

[2] *Frontline*, March 12, 'The Feel Good Factor', by P Sainath.
[3] BBC News, UK Edition (net version), 'India's Economy: Can the Boom Last?', January 7, 2004.

It is a fact that India's consuming class was consuming more and that the monsoons were good, and riding on the good rains was an economy booming, the corporate sector was also moving along with every centimeter of rain that fell on the Indian soil. The papers were filled with the IT sector notching up higher exports, that automobile sales had excelled previous levels and India's corporate sector was out shopping for foreign firms — a reversal of what large multinationals had done in India, or that Indian content films had a foreign audience.

The feel good story and the emphasis on the good had its genesis at an *ET (The Economic Times)* Awards function[4] where the then deputy prime minister, L K Advani suggested that if any one felt good, they had to be in India. As this specific report pointed out, "the retailing of the feel-good factor was apparent". What was significant, however, was that the media was doing the selling more than even the politicians.

As a media analyst pointed out, "It's like the US where the positives get more place than anything else. In fact, this was part of an agenda post-9/11."

Did he mean self-censorship? Yes.

This is an old American habit so entrenched in the print and television press but is new to the Indian set up. Part of the Indian media is going that way, he added and given that this section influences policy, it is significant!

Officials in some of the mainstream media houses claimed that the readers liked what they were seeing and circulation was on the rise. While this may be true, it was clear that the agenda to project India to urban Indians in only a favourable light was a selling game that was working. A Delhi-based theatre personality and educationalist while travelling on a Shatabdi

---

[4] *The Economic Times*, New Delhi, 'Feel Good Factor', Reshmi R. Dasgupta, February 2004.

train to Dehra Dun messaged (through a cellular mobile phone) that he had finished responding to most of his emails during the journey. The train had such a special service, "It feels good, India is shining," he said.

This is just one instance of the influence the media has.

Every social gathering in Mumbai or Delhi raved about India's progress and how the markets were doing (given the constant notional values put to the movement of the Bombay Stock Exchange sensitive index) or what is the latest in the vanity space — given the growing emphasis to this segment even in business dailies. And in many, if not most cases, the people talking about India's success story had little to do with it and were mere readers of the English press.

They hardly knew about the growing starvation in the country or that farmers had committed suicide due to the droughts and the lack of support from governments. *The Frontline* report[5] aptly puts into perspective the focus of the mainline media. It pointed out that a rural crisis through one full week accounted for just six news reports. But those covering the Lakme India Fashion Week were over 400. "Between them (the reports on the fashion week), they produced in one count, some 4,00,000 words in print," the report pointed out.

But such reporting had worked at two levels. The consuming urban middle class and the rich were getting caught in the flow of things and all that 'shined'. They were spending more and were enamoured by reports that said that they were much like the West, living off plastic money. Why stop consuming then after all the West knows better, is how Indians by and large respond.

At another level, the Western press was reading these reports and tuning in to India's print papers and fortunately, they were witness to real instances that gave some substance to the reports coming out of the Indian press. The outsourcing debate was a

---

[5] *Frontline*, March 12, 'The Feel Good Factor', by P. Sainath.

reality, so was the economic growth of 10.4 per cent or for that matter the over US $ 100 billion foreign exchange reserves or the growing interest in Hindi films in certain international markets.

According to a survey conducted by the India Brand Equity Foundation of a select list of journals including *Time Magazine*, *The Fortune*, *Business Week*, *The Economist* and *Newsweek*, there were over 200 articles on India during calendar year 2003. Of this, eighty-eight were positive and thirty-six in the general space. The 'outright negative' articles numbered fifty-six. The point is, India was up for debate and while positive developments drove the interest, every thing about the nation was being examined.

Even in 2004, *The Economist* had a cover on India and Thomas L. Friedman wrote a series of articles on India mostly from Bangalore, in the *New York Times*. And when the Congress emerged as the single largest party, just about every important publication across the globe had Sonia Gandhi on its cover. And as far as newspapers went, it was hard to count the number.

Notes Nitin Mantri, the client services director, Brodeur Worldwide, UK, "Sonia Gandhi and then Manmohan Singh were featured three days running on the front page of most national newspapers. It may have had something to do with the drama unfolding in 10 Janpath but it was more to do with the fact that India had emerged on the global scene and its leadership is critical to the West."

Well, then can we deny that the media, both in India and outside, have played an important role of changing the perception about India and adding relevant twists to what the nation is? The Indian media may have played to two galleries — the West and home, but it has done the job that though contentious, of forwarding the Indian case.

Now let us take a more focused look at the foreign media perception.

THIRD PARTY ENDORSEMENT

Khozem Merchant

A curious thing happened recently. *The New York Times* published a story on an Indian company. It was not just any story. In fact, it was not even a story that told of a business development such as an acquisition. It was an unremarkable story on the company's results.

Indian business has rarely commanded space in foreign newspapers. They were seen as small and parochial and of marginal interest to western readers. There have been exceptions. *The Financial Times* and *Business Week* have alone regularly reported Indian business. *The Asian Wall Street Journal* is improving. But what is the *NYT*, accustomed to grand coverage of state affairs, up to?

The *NYT*'s decision to widen its authoritative reporting of Indian political and social affairs to business — albeit confined to companies that export to the US — is notable. It heralds the foreign print media's recognition of the larger reporting environment in India.

For years, India's interface with the world in terms of news reporting was geo-political, in particular the troubled province of Kashmir. But a cessation of hostilities and the prospect of enduring peace between India and Pakistan raises an intriguing question: what will the contingent of expensive-to-maintain foreign correspondents in New Delhi, who subsist on geo-political news, do to fill their diet of coverage from the world's largest and most exotic democracy.

Fortunately, they have a choice. India's economy is booming.

In the past, India's economic fortunes, and economic news, may have been episodic. But this time the upturn seems to be enduring. More appealing is that bits of the economy have the world in their thrall.

That means a richer canvas for those media willing to shift their gaze to new competing interests. Topping this list is, of course, India's technology industry, whose global impact is introducing millions of foreigners to India.

By way of analogy, consider the US. The world's richest and most powerful country commands interest across the entire reach of its land, culture and politics because of its superpower status. These days it feels like that in India: India's technology industry is multiplying the level of interest in all aspects of the country.

So we see more in foreign newspapers about Bollywood — the Indian film industry. And also in business, whose global ambitions have burst forth after a decade of reform and repair, and is now evident in Indian companies' acquisitions of small western rivals. In effect, it is open season on coverage across India. And, scarcely believing their luck, foreign print media have had in the middle of all this an extraordinary Indian election to boot.

For the print media that have been ploughing a lonely furrow, the new situation is a windfall. Titles such as *The Economist, Business Week* and *FT* have an embracing worldwide view and capacity within their pages for a wide elasticity of Indian coverage.

The *FT* and *AWSJ* are the only daily global newspapers with a bureau in Mumbai. The weekly *Business Week* magazine also has a long-established bureau in the city — whose high property prices has been a major factor in holding back all but the most committed international publications. The dailies report the daily churn of business affairs, the piece-mean developments that an information-hungry global community demands. Now well ensconced, these titles also focus on secular business trends — the value coverage that educates and informs.

Technology may be foremost of these themes but given these titles' breadth, the scope of coverage has been gratifying wide. The *FT* has cast an eye on India's biggest business group in a lengthy analyses. The *AWSJ*'s tour de force on eating out in Asia included a modest but superlative eatery in an unfashionable part of Mumbai among its choice of top five restaurants in Asia. *The Economist* set aside its characteristic rigour for a look at the softer side of Bangalore, the IT capital, where young people have the incomes but not the time to enjoy it. *Business Week* asked why the same city's IT bosses were turning to advice from the new age guru, Sri Sri Ravi Shankar.

Nor are these excursions isolated. And, now, nor are these titles alone.

Many non-business titles have joined the queue. In the past few months, the *Sunday Times* of the UK has turned a new page in its India coverage, including a five page item on the human side of working in a call centre; twice as many pages on a feature about burning brides in Bangalore; the *NYT* visited a Parsee wedding in Mumbai, has exploited the convergence of the US election and the outcry on outsourcing of US jobs to India, and is now considering a full-time reporting presence in Mumbai.

A top newspaper in San Francisco — home to Silicon Valley (and thousands of Indian IT workers) — sent senior executives to India to examine opening a bureau — remarkable for a regional newspaper in the US. A group of journalists from the UK recently in Mumbai said they were working (sic) on how far the notion of outsourcing could be stretched — to dentistry, clothes, furnishings, God knows what else. As for travel writers on courtesy trips, they are legion in India.

The flip side of this supply is, of course, greater demand from editors in London, New York and numerous continental European cities. What this means is that more mid-level editors who once side-stepped India because of an institutional bias towards coverage of Western economies and cultures, now commission stories of a much more bread and butter character- alongside the coverage of the larger and more important news events from India.

In other words, India is mainstream.

My own newspaper, for example, has run stories on the problems of live-in chefs in Delhi, the toffs' school Doon, a tour around the bazaars and by-lanes of Mumbai, the same city's youngsters and their leisure time, and numerous profiles from Bollywood and the new emerging stars of television, business and technology.

This has important implications for a correspondent in Mumbai.

Until recently, this city paled besides New Delhi in terms of news value. But today, Mumbai is the point of entry for a new generation of India-watchers. Once, a Mumbai correspondent's advocacy to news-editors in the West to publish a story about a modest Indian company at the expense of a comparable one from the arguably higher-profile business community of Thailand, was a big challenge that ended in defeat.

Today, it is a doddle: the Indian wins.

The sea change in the editors' perception of India is coinciding with a structural shift-reform of foreign ownership of Indian print media.

The rules are divided into broad camps — news titles, in which foreign holding is capped at twenty-six per centre, and lifestyle titles, in which overseas parties may own up to seventy-five per cent. The *FT* has consummated a ten-year partnership with an Indian business title, while the *AWSJ* has tied up with India's biggest media group to publish its best- selling Asian edition in India. And the *Business Week* is hoping to formalize an arrangement with a Delhi-based group.

Conde Nast, the British magazine group, is scouting round for Indian titles to tap the huge rise of, and overseas interest in, the metropolitan classes; while the BBC's magazine division has gone a step further and launched a joint venture with *The Times of India* group.

India may be an emerging market but, it seems, it is no longer an emerging interest for the world's media.

LITTLE INDIAS

INDIA ABROAD

By now, the Indian abroad was noticeable and thriving on his professional successes. Who were they and what made them what they were or are, was a matter of curiosity for all those aware of the emerging power that Indians and India made up. No one assumed then, that is at the time of the advent, that an India flavour would find a place in different parts of the world. And this had less to do with the knowledge economy, acquisitions of foreign companies and creation of small multinational companies, a booming economy or cricket successes in Australia or Pakistan.

This was about Indian culture in the form of food, entertainment and dance. On hindsight, this was bound to happen as economic prosperity "automatically leads to cultural seepage and spillage into mainstream societies," points out Shridhar Subramanium, Sony Music India's chief executive officer. While saying this, it does not necessarily mean a love for or a need, it is a curiosity that can become habitual in that it is liked for what it is.

The India flavour, as one calls it, has lot to do with the younger lot of the twenty million expatriates that are running businesses or are part of business houses across the globe. While the overseas Indian has invested little back home as against China's fifty-five million who have been building that nation's foreign exchange reserves, their role has been crucial in spreading the native culture.

UK is the best, if not the only, example of India becoming part of the mainstream where Indian food is common and eaten by the British and Asians alike. Notes Nitin Mantri, client services director, Brodeur Worldwide, UK, based in London, "One can safely say that Chicken Tikka Masala comes close to being the national dish of the UK along with Fish and Chips. At last count, there were more than 28,000 Indian restaurants in the London area alone!"

And Indian films and music is commonly available now and the audience is not always Indian. It is often claimed, although refuted at times too, that Indians have now become a key contributor to London's economic set up. "The role is so great that even the Oxford Dictionary has incorporated a number of Indian words in its latest edition," says Farokh Balsara, a partner at Ernst & Young's Mumbai office in India.

The story of Indians in New York is different, yet to an extent similar as an Indian film at some of the best halls in that city is now not uncommon. Rajesh Jain, a partner at KPMG India suggests, "The demand is primarily coming from two levels, a cultural ethos mix where Indians that have grown up in the US and are missing their roots and those that have migrated to the US and long for Indian music and film. *Monsoon Wedding* and *Bend it like Beckham* have been success stories that has taken India beyond the non-resident Indians."

Even in Beijing, the India flavour is catching up with film and food making inroads into the Chinese mind and space. What is interesting here and is distinct from London, New York and Singapore is that the role of the expatriate is hardly visible. The curiosity has been created by a certain amount of intrigue and interest among local Chinese about Indian films, art, culture and food. What has also favoured the Indian emergence is the endorsement from the local government that is now working with the Indian government on improving relations. Given the autocratic political set up, the role of government has been considerable.

In Singapore, Indians have a significant presence in the corporate world and a little India does exist too. This presence has meant greater play in the region. According to Denny Kurien of Dow Jones in Singapore, Singapore already has a leading Indian education institution — the Bhavan's Indian International School and a second chain, the Delhi Public School was expected to open a branch when this section of the book was written. However, like other cities mapped in this section, Singapore has a keen interest in India's film and music world. It out bid Kuala Lumpur to host the International Indian Films Award, 2004 held in May. This indicated the relevance of the event to Singapore that has both to do with the business that the event brings in and Indian entertainment.

The significance of India's Bollywood and music comes out as an important aspect in driving the India flavour. Even in China, Hindi films make excellent gifts and if they are dubbed in local languages, then all the better. According to Subramaniam, it is Hindi films and therefore Hindi film music that is the key as it is "sufficiently kitsch and unique."

Of course, he adds: "You have bhangra meets hip hop genre that is emanating from the UK which is generating a certain coolness. This is truly an example of something Indian that is being developed by non-Indians — a sign of a culture that is vibrant and growing."

Balsara agrees that while the prime driver has been the film industry, there is a spillover. "Even in the US, Indian television programming is picking up. A similar trend is being seen in Singapore where television serials such as *Kyunki Saans Bhi Kabhi Bahu Thi* are being sold through the pirated market. There are many video parlours in the US that sell copies of the serial," he said. The size of the market is such that some of the television channels are considering beaming the programmes through satellite to the varied markets, he added.

The spillover goes beyond television serials and Hindi film music as other innovative sounds from India are generating interest. This has meant enhanced respect for Indian music companies. Sony Music India, for instance, now ranks among the top ten markets for its parent company. What has changed is that foreign labels are now writing in for experimental works and new ideas. "There is willingness from other countries to have a listen and see how to exploit the repertoire that we are generating," says the CEO of Sony Music's India operations. And this has a lot to do with what they see and here internationally.

India is for sure a curious market for any foreigner and the need to know and absorb is partly to do with the open mind of the West or the East, but mostly with what the Indian offering is. It is not surprising then that a beer and Indian *pulao* party occurs in US's Hartford, or a kebab night with Bollywood dancing happens in a home in London, or an Indian dance class is held regularly in Beijing or an Indian food festival is organized in Singapore.

The following chapter focuses on the space for Indians created by what they identify with in the cities of Beijing, New York, London and Singapore with writers familiar with these places penning down the India story abroad.

Let us look at China's Beijing to begin with.

CROSSING THE GREAT WALL

Pallavi Aiyar

After three decades of India and China sniffing at each other suspiciously with fair lashings of both pride and prejudice embittering relations, the last couple of years have finally seen a sweetening of this long sour relationship. The new emphasis has been on economic pragmatism, so that even as talks to resolve the touchy border disputes saunter along at a cautious diplomatic pace, bilateral trade is galloping. Business circles are abuzz with predictions of Sino-Indian trade volumes touching US $10 billion by the end of 2004.

However, it is not just in the economic arena that India is causing a stir in the middle kingdom, but in the often overlooked, yet tremendously significant realm of "soft power" as well. Joseph Nye, dean of Harvard University's John F. Kennedy School of Government, defines 'soft power' as — the influence and attractiveness a nation acquires when others are drawn to its culture and ideas. Soft power enables a nation "to achieve desired outcomes in international affairs through attraction rather than coercion."

Until very recently, soft power was largely an American monopoly in China. Mcdonald's golden arches beckon around virtually every street corner in major Chinese cities and Starbucks rear their green heads, even as colonel KFC looks benignly on. Pirated copies of Hollywood blockbusters flood the country's numerous DVD outlets and American brands flash prominently on shop fronts.

By contrast as recently as last June, the only thing notable about India in China, was the huge lacunae in information about its Himalayan neighbour, in the middle kingdom. Prior to the former Indian prime minister, Atal Behari Vajpayee's visit to the mainland towards the end of June 2003, I had spent an afternoon randomly quizzing Beijingers from different backgrounds about their perceptions of India. The answers ranged from the weird to the wary. Turbans, religion, poverty and natural disasters: these were the images that were talked about time and again. Other times, there was a long silence in response to my questions and I could see desperate brains working away to clutch at anything at all to say about India, only to come up empty handed.

But slowly, as the political vibes on both sides warm up and slick, business-suited economic ambassadors increasingly cross the border, brand India is undergoing somewhat of an image change, at least in the more urban, upwardly mobile areas of the mainland. The last year or so, has seen *desi*-style (local Indian-style) spicy food and classical traditions like yoga and Bharatnatyam gaining currency here, gradually transforming India from a non-entity to a player, in the soft power system in China.

"I am soooo interested in Indian culture," squeals twenty-year-old Cindy Liu, a third-year student of the Beijing Broadcasting Institute. "This year for my birthday I invited a friend to my favourite Indian restaurant in Beijing. He had never tried Indian food before, but he really liked it!" she continues.

While in India, Chinese food has long been a local favourite with chilly chicken and vegetable chowmein available even in roadside *dhabas* (restaurants), the Chinese have been more cautious in embracing Indian cuisine.

According to Mehrnoush Pastakia, Beijing's longest standing Indian restaurateur, when he first started his own restaurant in the Chinese capital some six years ago, there were barely three to four Indian eateries in Beijing and the clientele was almost exclusively expatriate. "I think the Chinese have a very strong indigenous food culture and suffered from many misconceptions about Indian food, like its excessive spiciness," he explains.

But cardamom-scented winds of change are blowing with some force. Four new Indian restaurants opened their doors in the capital in the last year itself and more and more of their customers are affluent, gastronomically adventurous Chinese. There are currently over a dozen Indian restaurants to choose from in Beijing, all doing brisk business. On Valentine's Day, Mehrnoush's Taj Pavilion was so full that he had to turn away several dozen couples in search of some rogan gosht to spice up their special evening. The Taj Pavilion has in fact now become a successful chain, with two branches in Beijing and a recently opened one in Xian.

In every translation, and food is no exception, a certain degree of deviation from the original is unavoidable. Just as in India, Chinese food has come to include paneer (cottage cheese) manchurian and like hybrids, that would undoubtedly cause the average Mr Lee to raise a sceptical eyebrow, Indian food in the Chinese capital would not go down particularly well with the typical Brahminical vegetarian. In keeping with Chinese tastes, beef and pork dominate the menus of many of the city's desi (local Indian) eateries, and aloo (potato) beef curries are quite the favourite.

"I love the way Indians cook beef," gushes Zeng Wei, an executive with a biotech company. "Although Chinese people are only now beginning to get to know about Indian food, I think one thing we (Chinese and Indians) have in common is that our cultures are very focussed on food!" she concludes.

When I first came to live in China in the fall of 2002, most often I was assumed to be a Pakistani. The only connections the average Chinese seemed to make with India were to do with dusty memories pulled out from a sepia-tinted past related to Raj Kapoor films; or even further back into the recesses of history, to Buddhism.

A year-and-a-half later, all manner of things Indian, suddenly seemed to have gained a visibility. In February of this year, the events section of *That's Beijing* magazine, the leading guide to the city, had India splashed all over it: India cultural month at a trendy salon; an Indian literary festival at a local library; a new yoga school featuring a Russian instructor of "Indian descent", and the opening of a new Indian restaurant.

Beijing's bustling bar street, Sanlitun, is almost outrageously cosmopolitan. A lone guitar player in a Texas cowboy-style hat strums the Eagles' mid-1970s hit track, *Hotel California* at the Nashville Bar. Across the road the Irish pub, Durty Nellies, stands next to the popular Belgian beer watering hole, the Hidden Tree. This year, finally saw India establishing a presence in this territory, sacred to Beijing's dedicated night life afficianados.

Every weekend through February and March of this year, Sanlitun's trendy Hart Salon, showcased aspects of Indian culture, including talks and demonstrations on Indian films, dance, and music; both contemporary and classical. The small space was packed to bursting for every event. As a graceful Chinese dancer demonstrated the intricacies of different Bharatnatyam *mudras*, almost a hundred, mostly young Chinese, looked on with rapt attention. Later, several enthusiasts made inquiries about joining Indian classical dance classes.

"I was really surprised at the great turn out," says Zang Jin, the owner of Hart Salon and chief organizer of the Indian festival. "But it is true that these days its very easy to find Indian handicrafts on the streets and a lot of people now like yoga and Indian food. Many people are now asking me where they can buy Indian movies and CDs," she smiles.

Zang explains that when she was growing up, Indian films like *Awara* and *Do Bigha Zameen* were very popular and people of her parent's generation watch them on DVD again and again, even today. However, for the younger crowd it is America that dominates their cultural imagination. "But now Chinese want to know about something else. Not just America and Hollywood all the time. India is such a colourful country and Indian women are so beautiful. I think if we had more exposure, India could also be very popular," she concludes.

Testament to this conclusion was the fact that originally Zang planned the Indian cultural festival as a one-month long affair. In the end, it extended to two months, with sections on yoga and Indian clothes added on. Simultaneously, Hart Salon became the space for the first ever privately organised exhibition of modern Indian art. Zang's friend Amitava Bhattacharya, an artist from Shantiniketan, together with her husband, Lao Dan, a Chinese artist, put together this exhibition, which included the works of a dozen painters from Shantiniketan.

Although appreciation of Indian art is still rare to find in China, one strong manifestation of Indian soft power in Chinese cities is the yoga craze that is sweeping across the young and beautiful who frequent China's health clubs and fitness centres. In the last year, several schools focussing exclusively on yoga have set up shop. One such school is run by an Indian yogi from Rishikesh, Mohan Bhandari. Set in the leafy environs of Beijing's centrally located Ritan park, Mohan's 'Yogi Yoga' centre has been a run-away success.

"People here (in China) are increasingly leading stressful lives and they need the spiritual relaxation that yoga brings. Other forms of exercise might keep you fit, but more and more Chinese need ways to ease the tension in their lives," says Mohan. Indeed, from the cheapest of community gyms to the poshest glass and chrome fitness centres, yoga classes are now considered de riguer among the health consciouss in China. But as Mohan has found out, many Chinese crave the 'authentic' Indian touch and are ready to pay for it. Such classes at Yogi Yoga cost between US $12-20 per session, which is not inexpensive by any standard.

"The Chinese teachers at the fitness centres are not so good. They are not able to tell us about the spiritual and philosophical underpinnings of yoga, like Mohan can," explains Wenfan Zhao, a young house wife who spends her afternoons perfecting gravity defying contortions under Mohan´s watchful eye. "Yoga helps me concentrate on my inner consciousness. Its changing my life," she says.

The Chinese appear in many ways to be starved for spirituality. Atheism was central to the Communist revolution and with the more recent crackdown on the religious sect, Falun Gong, there are few spaces for an average Chinese in which to express their spirituality openly. Yoga is the perfect answer. It is without overt religious connotations, yet is able to provide the spiritual sustenance sought by many young people.

Moreover, in China, yoga is being branded as trendy and youthful, giving the traditional Chinese Tai Chi, a run for its money. "I think only old people like Tai Chi," says thirty-two-year-old Liu Hong Yu, who is a recent recruit to the yoga fold. "Yoga is for us younger crowd. It is not only spiritual but it helps us look young and more beautiful."

For the moment, Mohan is the only Indian instructor in the Chinese capital, but several other schools advertise teachers of Indian descent or brandish the credentials of teachers who have studied in India under renowned yogis.

Capitalising on this yoga upsurge, a three-day festival of Indian literature in Beijing held in late February, attempted to lure people in, by organising a panel discussion on yoga and alternative health, as part of the event. Jayapriya Vasudevan, a literary agent and owner of the Jacaranda Press, feels that China is ripe for an introduction to Indian literature. Along with Alex Pearson, an expatriate library owner, she brought together over 400 titles of Indian writing in English, including fiction, travel writing and cook-books to put on display at Alex's 'Bookworm', library.

"Indian literature is so hot globally," says Jayapriya, "but in China there is still little knowledge about it. I am hopeful that this festival will begin the process of educating the market here, and I am encouraged by the response." Jayapriya has been in touch with several Chinese publishers and a few are now considering Indian writers.

However, at present, 'self-help' books on management, marketing and educational books involving learning English are what seem to interest most publishers, rather than fiction.

Featuring prominently among the works on display at the literature festival, were several books on Bollywood. Last year, *Lagaan* became the first Bollywood film to be released in China since 1994, when at that time a quota on the number of foreign films allowed to be imported into the mainland was established.

However, the popularity of the Raj Kapoor era films here in the immediate aftermath of the cultural revolution, persists till today, and the strong association people have with India and films has survived.

"The first Indian film I ever saw was *Awara*. I watched the songs, the dances, the beautiful actress Nargis; and I thought to myself then, 'how wonderful the world is,' remembers Ge Su, the director of the investment practice of a multinational consultancy firm in Beijing. He begins to drum his fingers on the polished table of the swanky conference room he is sitting in, and hums "*abala gu...hmmmm.*"

I nod my head encouragingly and join in, "*awara hoon...hmmm.*" It is a familiar moment. One that repeats itself with soothing regularity: in taxis flagged down by the Forbidden City, over jasmine tea sipped in courtly tea houses and during bumpy long-distance bus journeys.

Hindi films are the primary connection the average Chinese person makes with India. If in India the common perception of the Chinese until recently, was one of armies of inscrutable, chopstick-wielding Mr Wangs, dressed in blue Mao suits cycling energetically down, bicycle filled lanes; in China, the reverse stereotype that persists till today, is that Indians dance, sing and run around trees in beautiful clothes.

Although the last decade has seen Hollywood march inexorably on to the number one spot as far as foreign films in China are concerned, Hindi movies continue to generate considerable nostalgia amongst the thirty-five to fifty-five year age demographic. This is one reason why Indian dance schools are flourishing in Chinese cities.

Every weekend, dozens of eager parents flock to the C&M International Arts Education Centre in Beijing, dispatching their six to twelve year olds for Bharatnatyam and Kathak lessons from artiste Baohua Su. Su, who studied dance in India at the Kalakshetra University, has been teaching Chinese kids to *tillana* with elan for over a decade. She says that when she first started to teach, the majority of parents came to her after having watched the gyrations of Asha Parekh in *Caravan* or Da Peng Che as it was called in Chinese, which had been a smash hit in the mainland.

By contrast, today, many of China's well-heeled double income, one-child families are interested in the classical forms of the Indian dance repertoire. "Awareness of Indian classical dance has been slow to come, and compared to film dancing it is still not very high. But gradually, it is increasing," Su observes.

Compared to the power and weight of the American cultural engine, the influence of Indian culture in China remains minnow-like. Beef curries are no match for Big Macs and there are many Chinese who believe yoga originated in San Francisco. Moreover, the real significance of the 'cool' status that Indianess seems to be acquiring amongst urban Chinese is difficult to assess.

On the one hand, it is a superficial fashion, based on the appropriation of bits and pieces of the exotic. For most Chinese, the interest in things Indian, lies chiefly in their novelty value and they gravitate to those fragments of Indian culture that are colourful and fragrant, be these the incense sticks burnt during yoga meditation or the aromas of *masala chai*.

In China, the complexity and historical weight of Indian culture are neatly cut out and the remnants are served up in disconnected parcels as unreal and gauzy as an inserted song and dance 'dream' sequence out of a Bollywood extravaganza.

Nonetheless, despite the lack of depth and intricacy that lies behind the operation of Indian soft power, it remains 'a significant force in international relations. The attractiveness of a nation, even for reasons far too simplified for an academic's tastes, is a powerful weapon in its arsenal.

Thus, even as the average Chinese student bemoans America's hegemonistic power, it is significant that she may be simultaneously sipping a Mocha Frappacino freshly poured out at Starbucks, with slurping delight.

The popularity of a nation is not just based on the policies of its government but on its likeability in other arenas as well. As, Tarun Das, director general of the Confederation of Indian Industry (CII), an apex chamber of commerce in India, puts it, "Unless there is a broad emotional feeling about each other and appreciation of each other's customs and traditions, including food and clothes and films, it is difficult to do business easily."

Thus, the fact that India's cultural currency is discernably on the rise in the middle kingdom, is significant, however superficial this 'fashion' may be. The phenomenon is all the more weighty given that China has no Indian diaspora to speak of. Indians make up a titchy 300 of the 80,000 foreigners to which the capital, Beijing is host. For decades, the mental map of the average Chinese has had a blank spot to the south of the Himalayas. Gradually this spot is taking on shape and colour.

If soft power is seen as a diplomatic tool on par with economic and political ones, a little more energy spent on developing India's soft power across the border (disputed or otherwise) could go a long way.

Next on our trip is Singapore. The presence of Indians is nothing new but the perception, thought or view has transformed into an understanding of the space and relevance that Indians have in the functioning of Singapore.

The presence of Indians and their influence coupled with the emerging face of the nation in the global scenario has resulted in the Singapore government wishing to enhance its trade and economic ties with India. The first move in this direction was made in December 2003 through a proposal from the Singapore government that spelt out new ways of doing business between the two nations.

To understand where Indians stand and how they fit into Singapore, the following chapter flows from religion to business to entertainment and anything else that explains how the little India is not that little.

SINGAPORE, NOT JUST A LITTLE INDIA

Shibu Itty Kuttickal

Such devotion to Lord Murugan! A day of penance and thanksgiving that, at its simplest, take the form of a woman carrying a pot of milk and, at its most painful, the piercing of the skin, cheeks, or even the tongue, by 'vel' skewers.

Fire-walking. Self-flagellation. Hypnotic chants of "Vel, Vel"

Tamil Nadu, perhaps? Where else would you find such intense devotion to Vel Murugan?

Well, try Singapore. The city-state, where nearly ten per cent of the population is Indian has a district called 'Little India' where Indian devotees of Sri Murugan converge in the early days of February for the Thaipusam festival. Visit this district during Thaipusam and you'll see how deep-rooted Indian traditions are in this modern metropolis.

Or, check out Kuala Lumpur, yet another modern city, the capital of Muslim-dominated Malaysia, during the same period and you will experience the same feeling. The festival is proof that such traditions are not easily stifled by a surge in modernism.

And, it is a well-known fact that over ninety per cent of the population in the island of Bali — a popular tourist destination — consists of Hindus.

Another community, the Malayalee Syrian Christians belonging to the marthoma church managed to pool their resources to build a beautiful church last year. And, one Sunday every month, they have a worship service in the Malayalam language, although the generation of Singaporean-born church members prefer the English service.

In both Singapore and Malaysia, other Christian denominations, especially among the Tamil and Malayalam-speaking communities, have worship services in their own language.

Indians in Southeast Asia have a long history. The Balinese believe that Hinduism was brought to the island by Indian traders about two centuries ago.

On the other hand, the nucleus of the people of Indian origin in Singapore was formed by those who were with Sir Stamford Raffles, the East India Company officer who arrived in Singapore in 1819 to establish a base for arranging provision and protection for the company ships carrying cargo between India and the region, especially China.

They consisted of 120 soldiers and several assistants and domestic servants. For nearly forty-eight years from 1825, Singapore, as a penal colony, saw an influx of Indian convicts, who were utilised virtually as slave labourers to clear swamps and jungles and in the construction of roads and buildings. From 1830 onwards, Indians, mostly Tamil, were brought in as indentured labour to work on plantations, civic projects and construction of government and military facilities.

Also around this time, began the influx of Indian traders — such as the Sindhis, the South Indian Muslims, the Chettiars — who were attracted by Singapore's growing status as a trading hub. As the territory continued developing, it attracted more and more Indians in search of white-collar jobs. The migration of Indians gained momentum after the Second World War and the Partition of India. But fresh influx virtually ceased in the 1950s as Singapore started controlling immigration.

Indians have evolved to become an indelible presence in these societies. At the same time, they have blended seamlessly into the social fabric.

In the 1960s and '70s, the top posts in the civil service, the judiciary, the armed forces and educational institutions were held largely by the Indians. Indians had a head start in the civil service and professions, because of their general proficiency in English.

Now people of Indian origin are represented in all sectors of Singaporean economy and society to a much greater extent than the indigenous Malay community. Indians hold important positions of power. S.R. Nathan, Singapore's president is of Indian descent and so also are four ministers in the government headed by Prime Minister Lee Hsien Loong, who took over from Goh Chok Tong recently.

People of Indian descent are contributing to a large extent to the efforts of the government to build up a vibrant commercial hub in Singapore.

The city-state, which offers a high-tech working environment and excellent living conditions, is a happy hunting ground for Indian information technology professionals.

Business Acumen

Furthermore, the contributions of Indian businessmen are noted all over the region. Two names come to mind immediately: Thakral and Mustafa.

Kartar Singh Thakral, a devout Singapore-based Sikh who is known to spend considerable time every day at the gurdwara, is at the helm of a dynamic multibillion dollar business empire spanning 25 countries and employing over 8,000 people. His father, Sohan Singh Thakral, had migrated to Thailand as a ten-year-old and had a humble beginning — hawking clothes on the streets of Bangkok.

And in Singapore's Little India, the haphazard layout and product display at a retail store disguise a business that rakes in over $ 300 million in annual sales. The raja of retail in Little India, Mohamed Mustafa & Shamsuddin, or just Mustafa, as

The sun is not setting but rising, as India draws on the energy of the sun to bridge gaps
between development and the underdeveloped.

Changing time — keeping pace with a faster world.

Waiting for the sun to shine — a lady walking several kilometers to get water.

Ironing out problems that reflect India.

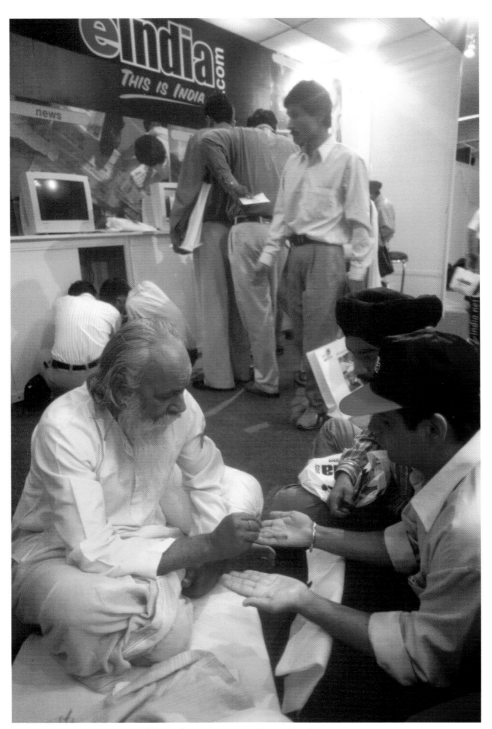

Many futures being determined here.

Mobility reaching the heartland.

The changing face of globalization.

Different ideologies, sharing space.

Tourists coming in — the curiosity grows.

the outlet is popularly known, had its beginnings from an itinerant peddler by name Haji Mohamed Mustafa. Once he had laid the foundation, his son, Mustaq Ahmad, took it to greater heights.

Rooted in Indianness

Indian culture has been kept alive in Singapore. While Indians, as a community, have imbibed the modernity of the societies they are living in, there is a distinct 'Indianness' about them that can be felt in their homes, businesses and whichever fields of activity they are involved in on a daily basis. Singapore Indians are largely local-born and linked to India primarily through the continuation of the cultural traditions rather than by any nationalistic feelings.

Many of them have no personal connections in India. But Indian traditions have proved quite hard to be uprooted.

Those born and brought up in Singapore look upon themselves as Singaporeans rather than Indians. Yet, you do find women with turmeric paste on their faces when you visit Indian homes in these parts.

There is, however, a charge that Indians coming in to the region are bringing in their own 'baggage' of prejudices. Some say the 'baggage' is slightly in excess. The fracas over Indian information technology professionals being mistreated by the Malaysian police in March 2003, brought to the fore such an interpretation. Some of these people are said to have tried to form an expatriate pressure group to tackle a issue of poor wages. They withheld labour, but many of them did not realise that this automatically cancelled their work permits. Their employers retaliated and tipped the police. Raids followed, which, unfortunately, got a bit out of hand.

This interpretation implies that when the IT boys and girls, with dreams in their eyes, land in Southeast Asia, they bring in some social habits that the culturally-diverse people in ASEAN (the Association of Southeast Asian Nations) countries find abusive, annoying and sometimes, abhorrent.

But, at the same time, some local and naturalised Indians in the region seem to have a habitually combative attitude towards immigrants from India. Wrote Sunanda K. Dutta-Ray, former editor of *The Statesman*, Calcutta, in one of his columns to Singapore's *The Straits Times* newspaper: "Many locally-born Indians, whether in Singapore or Malaysia, have chips on their shoulders the size and weight of the Qutab Minar."

The Ties that Bind

Generally, however, what comes out while talking to a cross-section of the Indian population in Singapore is a groundswell of goodwill for their country of origin. There is this generation of old-timers who always wanted to return to India, but were forced by circumstances to stay put. They continue to have familial and friendship connections with India and fly back once in a while to renew these ties.

This goodwill remains among Indians born and brought up in the region, though tinged with some frustration at the perceived slow pace of change in India as brought out in a conversation with a friend of Indian origin George Samuel — a Singapore citizen who married an Indian girl from Bombay and has been visiting India on and off. "The true potential of India is being stifled by the corruption in the country and the inept politicians," he says.

He remembers the cultural shock he experienced as he visited Bombay for the first time — the Dharavi slums, the beggars and the prostitutes residing alongside the skyscrapers of the commercial capital. It took some time for him to digest these sights. What he saw then, he says, was two nations and for him, nothing much has changed over the past three decades.

He sees a country full of loafers, which he finds difficult to comprehend as he compare them with the industrious Indian workers back home. "There must be something about the system in India that is affecting productivity. Unless this is addressed, the country will not be able to prosper," he says.

Samuel's recent visits to India has not changed his overall view of the country drastically. He agrees that global perceptions of India are changing and that internationally, India is being viewed as a market to watch. Yet, the ground realities leave a lot to be desired, says Samuel.

Samuel's view does not, however, seem to be the mainstream opinion. Most Indians in Singapore talk about the rapid welcome changes in India and the country's growing profile internationally. There is the realisation that things are changing, albeit slowly.

An Emerging Asian Power

This change in the mainstream opinion on India has been gradual, but real. The dramatic nuclear tests, the quickening pace of economic growth, the turnaround in India's foreign exchange reserves, the highly qualified and efficient information technology workforce from the country, all have contributed to the qualitative change in perceptions on India.

The spectre of a great Indian collapse has passed, yielding to a vision of an India emerging as an Asian power to claim its rightful place alongside Japan and China. The sight of the mushroom clouds in the desert in Rajasthan as India announced its nuclear capability in 1998 had served to place the country to be viewed in a different light.

It has often been noted in conversations with knowledgeable Indians here that the country possesses the world's third largest army. Its importance is underscored by the country's strategic position at the crossroads of the Persian Gulf, Central Asia and Southeast Asia. There were whispers about a growing Indian influence as New Delhi, in 1998, announced the formation of a new Far Eastern Command of its navy, that was intended to give it a far greater reach in Southeast Asian waters. All these have helped to lift the stature of India all over the world and has certainly rubbed off on the Indian diaspora.

And people keep travelling to India and bring back positive stories of change and reforms in the country. Singapore Airlines and its subsidiary, Silkair, have been adding and continue to add to their Indian destinations.

According to P.N. Balji, a Singapore-born Indian who was the founder editor of *Today*, the rival free newspaper to the highest-circulated Singapore daily, *The Straits Times,* there are definite and discernible changes in India.

Balji, fifty-seven, whose parents were from Kannur and whose wife is from Mahe, travels at least once a year to Kerala. Some twenty years ago, he wrote in the Singapore tabloid, *The New Paper,* which he edited before founding *Today,* about the lack of basic infrastructure and the corruption prevailing in India, as experienced by him in his travels across the country. He, however, expressed happiness, as he talked to me recently, over a definite change in the attitudes among the Indian people and the improvement in the facilities as he found in his recent journeys from Singapore to Cochin and beyond.

Such changes in perception among opinion makers are trickling down into the mainstream public opinion in the region and is generally leading to a favourable sentiment towards India.

There are a lot of positive noises being made about India in the region. The image of a land of casteist, communal and class struggles with an environment that is hostile to business and where corruption rules and poverty is rampant has now given way to a new image — that of a nation that is soaring and is occupying a valid place in the international arena.

There is appreciation and admiration — sometimes grudging — of the professionalism in management shown by Indian corporates and there is a surging interest in the arts and culture of India.

Indian Flavour is in

An analysis of the content of Singaporean newspapers would also bear out that Indian flavour is in. There have been occasions when the Indian High Commission reacted to negative coverage. But the fact remains that the coverage of Indian political and economic news has increased by leaps and bounds and it has been mostly positive.

The coverage of the Indian arts and cultural scene, especially news about Bollywood, has also increased. Indian movies have had a tremendous following in Southeast Asia, especially in Malaysia, Indonesia and Thailand.

Meanwhile, there is a growing realisation, as reflected in the regional media, that, against all odds, the Indian democratic institutions have functioned credibly and have attained a certain maturity over the last fifty-seven years.

For instance, *Today*, in a commentary written by staff writer Shobha Tsering-Bhalla, painted the 2004 Indian elections as a victory of secularism by pointing out that with the defeat of the Bharatiya Janata Party and the National Democratic Alliance that it led, the nation was poised to have a Christian prime minister in Sonia Gandhi working with a Muslim president, Dr. A.P.J. Abdul Kalam. Obviously, this commentary was written before Sonia Gandhi refused to take the post. But that did not take away the positive light being thrown on Indian developments by the media here.

Tsering-Bhalla, an Indian resident here, opines that whichever government may come to power in New Delhi, the economic reforms that have been set in motion, would continue. And this statement and realistic prediction, as it has turned out to be going by the statements of the current incumbent in New Delhi, is of interest to business in Singapore that is waiting to take economic ties forward. It can't be forgotten that companies such as Singapore Telecom and Changi Airport are waiting to invest more in the subcontinent.

It must have been such confidence in the stability of the Indian governmental edifice that prompted Singapore to press, in 2003, for a Comprehensive Economic Cooperation Agreement (CECA) with the Indian government. The CECA, which has been delayed because of the Indian elections, would create a free-trade zone between the two countries, an open-skies pact that would lead to unimpeded air links, promotion of investment and education initiatives and other steps to integrate Singapore economy with that of India.

Such moves have prompted a rethink by investors also.

Recently, Aberdeen Asset Management launched the India Opportunities Fund — a fund for investing in the Indian stock market — for investors in Singapore. The response to the fund was overwhelming. Fund manager Devan Kaloo told this writer recently that nearly $70 million flowed into the fund within five weeks of the launch of the fund. He said nearly fifty per cent of this came in from the investors' CPF funds, which meant that the confidence in India was so great that investors were willing to put in their hard-earned money into the country.

The interest in the Indian resurgence has had its effect in other areas too. For example, in cinema, Bollywood is obviously the current rage. Malaysia and Singapore have welcomed Indian filmmakers to base their productions in their countries.

The International Indian Film Academy's annual extravaganza was held in the Genting Highlands of Malaysia in 2002. There was tough competition between Malaysia and Singapore to host the event in 2004 and Singapore won in the end. It would appear that almost all of the Bollywood glitterati had descended on Singapore for the event held during the third week of May. It also saw a tremendous response from the Indian diaspora from all over the region and beyond. Most of the seats were sold out nearly a month before the event!

In cultural terms, the Indians are the most diverse of Singapore's ethnic communities. About sixty-four per cent of the Indian community is of Tamil origin and Tamil is one of the four official languages, together with Chinese, Malay and

English, in Singapore. The other distinct Indian communities are Malayalees (about eight per cent), Punjabis (seven per cent), Sindhis (six per cent) and Gujaratis (two per cent).

Indians are also the most religiously diverse of Singapore's ethnic categories: fifty to sixty per cent Hindus, twenty to thirty per cent Muslims, twelve per cent Christians, seven per cent Sikhs and one per cent Buddhists. All these groups are active in their respective religious circles too.

Yet, there is a feeling among the Indian diaspora that India remains a grey zone for most of the Southeast Asian political, cultural and intellectual elite, including those of Indian origin. Of course, by its sheer size, the country cannot be ignored. But it doesn't seem to be that successful or threatening, neither is it that exotic, to warrant more than some placating or cordial statements.

Many are bewildered by the paradox of articulate Indian diplomats and intellectuals, on the one hand, and the country's economic weakness — as brought out by the negative vote by the rural Indian poor against the BJP in the 2004 elections — on the other.

The diaspora Indians have made a mark in the region by sheer dint of hard work. And, they have contributed their mite in trying to bring about a change of attitude towards their country of origin. Most nations don't like foreigners, but in Singapore they realize that there is no foreigner like the Indian.

Let us move right across the globe to New York city in the US — the land many Indians want to visit.

India, for the American, has till recently, been an unknown territory and an un-chartered one too. The myopic American typically struggled to develop an understanding of who Indians are and where they come from. With Americans hardly travelling even within their own country, the inability to get a grip or appreciate any other nation and its people was bound to be hard for them.

It is in this perspective that India's growing presence should be seen.

A BITE INTO THE BIG APPLE

Vivek Rai

Cultural imperialism is a term we have come to understand well in India, as in much of the east; too simplistically defined as the slow displacement of local cultures by the capitalistic west. But for those of us who live on the other side of the world, in the United States, there is a new kind of cultural trade taking place. And while it lands very short of being called imperialism, it has made some Americans more aware of India than ever before.

This doesn't necessarily translate into another term that the Indian media tends to use fairly liberally — that India 'has arrived' in America. We Indians tend to get excited very easily by the smallest notice taken of us by the West. A few months ago, as I surfed the internet for news on India, I came across the front page of *The Times of India*, boldly announcing that actor Rahul Bose had been chosen by *Time* Asia magazine as India's alternative hit-maker.[1] A newsworthy item, possibly, but certainly not for the front of the paper's home page.

And so, here in America, India is on the radar, but it has a long way to go before it permeates into the lives of ordinary Americans beyond New York and other big cities that have attracted the South Asian immigrant. Unless you take into account the debate on out-sourcing, which currently best

---

[1] *The Times of India*, October 27, 2003.

defines India right now, and at least as far as the US media is concerned.

CNN's Lou Dobbs' Exporting America series has literally made a campaign against Indians who are taking away jobs from 'decent hard-working Americans'. John Kerry has made outsourcing a significant focus of his campaign against George W. Bush. Television screens flash images of protest marches by laid off workers who have lost their jobs to cheaper labour overseas; and reams of paper is dedicated to stories of "how I trained junior colleagues from India, and subsequently found myself out in the cold".

If the economic prophets of doom are to be believed, then it is India, not the 'axis of evil' that is enemy number one. A random search on the web reveals web sites like *www.yourjobisgoingtoindia.com* and *www.nojobsforindia.com* that serve as diatribes against companies that have sent jobs out of the United States.

The latter web site for example, holds up a warning sign against outsourcing, saying 'This isn't a shirt or a toy, this is your bank account, credit and personal information in a foreigner's hands. How easy would it be for terrorists to get this information? Would a non-American think twice about selling this information to the wrong person?"

In the current atmosphere of fear and tension against terrorism, these are apt words meant to reach out to the core of the American heartland, combining economic deprivation with the fear factor.

Another site, *www.techsunite.org,* has an Offshore Tracker that monitors the number of jobs that are leaving the US, and lists the companies responsible (under Top 10 Culprits). According to this web site, Americans lost 160,785 jobs over a three-year period between April 2001 and April 2004. (Another research group Global Insight claimed in a study released in March 2004 that while 104,000 U.S. jobs were lost because of offshore outsourcing between 2000 and 2003 — some 35,000 a year — more than 90,000 U.S. jobs were created last year due to the cost savings reaped by employers who sent IT work overseas.)

Wired magazine, in its February 2004 cover story (*The new face of the silicon age*) cites a number of research reports echoing doomsayer beliefs; one by the research firm Gartner states that one in ten US technology jobs will go overseas by the end of 2004; another, by Forrester Research claims that "in the next fifteen years, more than 3 million US white collar jobs, representing US $136 billion in wages, will depart to places like India, with the IT industry leading the migration."

Contrast this with rising awareness of other things Indian stateside. The March 25 issue of *Time Out New York*, the city's definitive guide to the week's events in the Big Apple, had a cover announcing "Bollywood on Broadway" with Ayesha Dharker and Anisha Nagarajan, the stars of the Andrew Lloyd Webber musical *Bombay Dreams*, against a backdrop of the Taj Mahal, (which incidentally happens to be in Agra).

Inside was a fourteen page South Asian New York Special, featuring the latest and the hippest in Ayurveda, design, cinema, and music.

There was a poll asking New Yorkers to vote for the name of a big city in India (the choices, Bombay or Mumbai, thereby implying a familiarity with history and current events). There was a profile of DJ Rekha, whose Basement Bhangra nights (the first Thursday of every month) at SOBs, a downtown nightclub has become one of the city's most happening parties. Other profiles included those of Brooklyn based writer Amitav Ghosh, the queer friendly Desilicious parties hosted by Sholay Productions, and the best in Indian cuisine.

Or consider if one wants to go and see a Bollywood film. Some cities across America, including New York, have Indian film screenings in neighbourhood cinemas in the primarily South Asian dominated districts; for example, in New York it's the Eagle Cinema in Jackson Heights, often referred to as 'Jaikishen' Heights. The Eagle promises a throwback to the pre-multiplex cinema culture of Indian theatres, much like the

Regal in New Delhi's Connaught Place, complete with broken seats, noisy children and an interval for *samosa* and *chai*.

But for those New Yorkers too faint-hearted to endure the movie watching experience, *desi* style, there is now an alternative.

In the heart of the city, in the fabled, neon glaring Times Square, the Virgin Mega-Store shares space with a multiplex that shows Indian fare at least one week every month in on of its theatres, alongside the latest Hollywood blockbusters. *Devdas*, *Lagaan* and even the lesser known *Agnivarsha* found their way to this theatre, and the audience at these screenings was not just the loyal South Asian diasporas; the foreigners were very much in presence as well, soaking in the *masala* charms of Bollywood, aided by sub-titles.

No small feat considering that most other foreign language films rarely step outside the boundaries of art-house screening rooms.

Are these then signs that Indian culture might be making its way onto the American mainstream's cultural radar, in much the same way that Chinese dim sum, Japanese Sushi and Cuban (via Puerto Rico) salsa?

It's too early to tell.

What is a more interesting question to pose is whether the co-opting of the aforementioned things into American culture has given people in this country any great understanding of Chinese, Japanese or Cuban culture?

Alpa Patel, a Media Studies student of Indian origin, born and brought up in the US, points out that while there is an increasing influence of things Indian on the American market, it hasn't necessarily translated into a deeper understanding of India among people. "Americans are good at co-opting things to fit in to their own mould, and there is a fascination with the exotic elements of India, be it in terms of food, fashion or music; but the average American is not anymore aware of the politics or culture of India; he or she is just looking at another American product, not where it came from."

Sreenath Sreenivasan, founder of the South Asian Journalists Association, notes that even if there is a degree of awareness, it remains to be seen where it will lead to. "Over the years, certain communities become hot and then fade away. Will India stay hot? We don't really know."

One way or the other, it is an exciting moment to be involved in the arts as far as India is concerned. There are at least three art galleries in New York that devote themselves solely to selling art from the Indian subcontinent.

Bombay Dreams' arrival on Broadway this year was preceded with the huge commercial successes of *Monsoon Wedding* and *Bend it like Beckham*. While neither of them was Indian (the former was American produced, the latter British) their popularity helped add momentum to the already growing demand for *desi* music in the city's nightspots, on the music television channels and advertising.

Sabrina Dhawan, who wrote the screenplay for *Monsoon Wedding* while a student at Columbia Film School in New York, notes, "In the film world a few years ago, when I made my short film *Saanjh*, there wasn't much keenness to fund projects related to India, especially if they were set there. Now, while there is still some resistance, a lot of people in Hollywood are more open to exploring possibilities regarding India."

A prime example being Dhawan's collaborator on *Monsoon Wedding*, director Mira Nair, whose latest venture *Vanity Fair* has liberally used Indian settings and music to add to the movie's international appeal. And the growing number of television advertisements that use the sitar or tabla as background music to sell their products, none of which have anything to do with India (such as hamburgers).

Add to that the trend towards buying Indian design jewellery, the art of *mehendi* and of course the *bindi* (promoted by No Doubt lead singer Gwen Stefani and Madonna). But again, it needs to be reiterated here that most of these are taken out of their original cultural contexts, and in many ways become the background to American marketing's foreground.

The one exception to this could possibly be India's biggest export to the west, yoga. Swami Vivekananda at the Columbian Exposition World Fair in Chicago first introduced this ancient regimen to the Americans in 1893. But it didn't catch on. Then, in the 1960s, it was picked up by the hippie generation as part of its alternative and possibly more spiritual lifestyle. By the late 1970s and into the '80s, yoga faded once more, unable to cope with the latest fad in aerobic exercises, represented by the likes of Jane Fonda and Richard Simmons.

But in the last few years, there has been a mass scale resurgence of yoga, fuelled by celebrity endorsements by the likes of Sting, Tina Turner, and most importantly Madonna, who publicly traded in her dumb-bells for the yogic posture. Four years into the new century, yoga learning and practice centres have mushroomed all over the country; and despite having lived in India for twenty-nine years, I am often caught off-guard by how some Americans know much more about yoga's philosophy than I do.

This also happens to be the time that the second generation of Indians is coming of age, and contributing to the cross-cultural influences of the West with India. The parents of this generation were immigrants who came into this country in the 1960s, taking advantage of the Immigration Act or Hart Cellar Act of 1965, that abolished national origin quotas that had been in place since 1882; immigrants were to be admitted on the basis of their skills and professions rather than their nationalities. A flood of Indians made their way across the seas to carve out new lives for themselves, often in tiny towns in the middle of nowhere (the current debate on granting of H1-B and L1 visas is reflective of that continuous stream).

And it seems to be the rising visibility of this new generation of South Asians that are helping spawn the rise in media attention. Many of this generation are in their twenties and thirties, professionally successful, striking out in the creative arts rather than the traditionally preferred careers of medicine, banking and technology. The surfeit of Indo-Americans films that have appeared and quickly disappeared is testament to the fact that while commercial and critical success may still be wanting, there are still a whole lot of new voices out there articulating their cross-cultural identities onto the national dialogue.

As a regular subscriber to *The New Yorker*, one of the country's foremost weekly magazines, it's been interesting to see the number of 'Indian' writers whose work has appeared in its fiction pages (between April and June 2004, Jhumpa Lahiri, V.S. Naipaul and Hanif Kureishi all made the cut, though not all their writing was Indo-centric).

A couple of years ago, I began subscribing to an email listing of daily news and feature stories related to South Asia in the American print and internet media. What caught my attention was the number of stories not from the big news corporations, the *New York Times, Washington Post* etc., but reports on India, the food, the culture and the politics, in the smaller newspapers and web sites like Grand Forks Press, Phoenix Business Journal and such. *www.fortwayne.com*, a tiny newspaper and website company in Indiana carried a front-page story on the violence that marred the start of the India's general election.[2]

So it's a complicated set of affairs. There is probably more influence of Indian culture on Americans than ever before; but we're a far cry from being on the national consciousness of the world's richest country. According to Arvind Rajagopal, journalist and professor at New York University, "The idea that true recognition is finally beginning to dawn is misleading. Rather, it inaugurates a new phase of a relationship, where a new set of mutual understandings and misunderstandings are both at work. It would therefore be important to know what these are, and how they might interact with each other."

Coming of age as I did in the post-liberalization period in India, I grew accustomed to debates about how American

---

[2] http://www.fortwayne.com/mld/fortwayne/news/local/8488536.htm

culture was invading our lives, through the idiot box, food, fashion, language and attitude.

Over a decade later, as I write this article sitting in a high rise building in Manhattan, the seat of the American Empire, it's a nice feeling to know that at least a slice of India is making its presence felt on these shores. It's not enough to make curry the most popular dish among this country's denizens, but it's a start. After all, in the words of a *desi* cab driver who took me home one late, party night "New York or New Delhi, India is everywhere".

This is our last stop — London — a city that has so many Indians that a touring Indian could think he is back home and forget that he were in a foreign nation but for the gloomy and unpredictable British weather.

Indians in London go back a long way when India's Green Revolution made the Punjab farmer rich owners of productive farm land. Many sold out and spent their money on migrating to the land of the Angrez (English). The Indian then could not bring enough English words to his lips to structure a simple sentence. The jobs they held were usually at the lower end of any hierarchy and their profile was not much to write home about.

A slow struggle up the social ladder, the Indians quietly went about changing the way they lived and were being seen. From corner shop owners to restaurateurs to prosperous second-hand car dealers to marketing executives to IT specialists to PR executives or steel barons like the Mittals or the multidimensional Hindujas, the Indians were making their way.

But the past two years has seen the strides grow larger and the Indian enter the mainstream be it food, entertainment, business or culture. This may explain why Selfridges, one of the Britain's leading upmarket departmental stores organised a theme month on India, notes Nitin Mantri, client services director with Broeder's London office. "Indian cuisine, clothes by leading Indian designers and films from Bollywood (with the Big B, Amitabh Bachchan personally signing the K3G DVD) were on display," Mantri added.

Is India ruling London? It is too early to say, but the mainstream is aware that the stream is mainly India, if one may be a bit presumptuous!

THE INDIAN RAJ

Ben King

Asweaty gym outside a shopping centre in Bayswater might not be the first place you'd look for a troupe of Bollywood dancers. But if you come at 8:15 on a Wednesday, that's exactly what you will find.

Vandana Alimchandani and her colleagues teach seven classes a week in dance studios and gyms across the capital. Londoners from a range of nationalities study dance to a mix of *bhangra* and Bollywood tunes. She also has a troupe of fifteen performers who do public events and weddings, and she's auditioning thirty more.

"It's something I have been doing for ten years," she says. "But I decided to take it mainstream four years ago."

Dancers in London have highly eclectic tastes — you can study anything from Viennese waltzes to Brazilian *capoeira*. That's one of the reasons her classes have an appeal, says Alimchandani. "It's not a style you get trained in. It takes in a bit of everything — Arabian, Latin, and street styles."

But interest in Bollywood has been growing gradually, she says, and it really took off a few years ago. "(The musical) *Bombay Dreams* came out, a lot of Bollywood films came out on general release, Channel 4 had a Bollywood season," she says. "Everything spurred up into a real peak of interest."

Bombay Dreams certainly sparked off a fashion for all things Bollywood. But Britain and India, two tea-drinking democracies with a love of cricket and the English language, have a deep-seated relationship that dates back centuries.

Nonetheless, Britons are finding themselves more and more in touch with India every day. In ten years, the cost of a telephone call to India has declined to a fraction of what it once was. An email costs virtually nothing. And it's cheaper than ever to fly between the two nations. So many Britons find themselves calling Delhi or Bangalore to check their bank balance or book an airline ticket.

So has this new closeness changed the way Britons look at India?

When *Bombay Dreams* came out, you could be forgiven for thinking that it had. Certain high-brow elements sneered at this production, as it was the brainchild of Andrew Lloyd-Webber, a man who brings out the British hatred of successful people powerfully. It became the theme of the summer nonetheless. And the composer A.R. Rahman certainly managed to raise his own profile on the back of *Bombay Dreams*. In fact, this year, Rahman is conducting a couple of concerts of Indian movie themes with the City of Birmingham Symphony Orchestra.

This possibly led to Selfridges, one of London's top department stores, running a big Bollywood promotion, and the Victoria and Albert museum put on an exhibition of Indian movie posters.

Despite this wave of popularity, Bollywood movies still aren't widely appreciated beyond the art-house cinema crowd and the diaspora communities. The song-and-dance numbers still seem a trifle odd to a British public. They can happily accept intergalactic warfare and zombie invasions in their films, but still find it a little odd when action heroes break into song.

There are signs that the Bollywood invasion may have reached its limits, at least for the moment. A recent tour of England by Aishwarya Rai and Hrithik Roshan failed to sell out some of the venues. But then this may be because of an overdose.

But in terms most Britons' experience of Indian culture this is just the icing on the cake. Or more accurately, the crisped onions on the *biryani*.

In 2001, Robin Cook famously declared that chicken tikka masala was the national dish. Of course, this frighteningly scarlet concoction doesn't really count as Indian. It was invented in England to satisfy the desires of the British palate. Legend has it that a can of Campbell's soup featured in the original recipe. And many of the chefs who serve them up today will be Bangladeshis.

But the Indian influence on the British palate dates long before the curry house boom of the1970s. The classic Victorian breakfast dish, kedgeree, a mix of fish, eggs and raisins in saffron rice, is one example. And this writer's own grandmother was regularly cooking curries even before the Second World War!

The Indian subcontinent has had a dominant hold on the less expensive end of the British restaurant scene for years. Every small town now has its Koh-i-Noor tandoori or a Taj Mahal. Millions of Britons have been rescued from a life of unremittingly bland dining by these heroic restaurateurs, working long hours on tiny margins.

Much though it is loved, the 'ruby murray' (as it's known in rhyming slang) has suffered something of an image problem. Indian restaurants have traditionally been seen as a place for hungry drunks. Many restaurants serve a dish called the phaal. Packed with chillies and edible only after many lagers, it is served to punters who insist on the hottest dish on the menu.

If you wanted classy dining, French food was top of the pecking order. But recently a number of Indian restaurants have won the seal of acclaim from the bible of French culinary taste — A star rating from the Michelin Guide.

Two restaurants, Zaika (flavour) and Tamarind, have achieved the coveted accolade, and a clutch of others are bidding to join them.

Cinnamon Club, in the old Westminster Library, is right next to the House Of Commons. So many members of parliament and government workers, who have access to several excellent canteens but few gourmet restaurants within walking distance, have become devotees, swapping gossip over the tandoori halibut and sandalwood chicken breasts.

Michelin stars perhaps promise to boost the status of Indian food in Britain, and may perhaps encourage restaurants lower down the price scale to put more emphasis on fresh, quality ingredients and less on food colouring and ghee (Indian cooking medium).

A recent survey of the nation's curry houses found alarming levels of colouring materials such as tartrazine and ponceau 4R — hardly traditional ingredients. But the media storm that followed this discovery showed just how important the curry is in Britain's national life.

Nonetheless, British diners owe their curry houses an enormous debt for spicing up the nation's diet. Will offshore call centres and software houses spice up these other areas of Britain's service economy?

For British corporations, the proposition is almost irresistible. Britons view call centre jobs as at best a tedious McJob, if not a latter-day equivalent of Blake's Dark Satanic Mills. With high staff turnover and poorly motivated workers, companies struggle to reduce costs and keep staff turnover low. In India, they say, they find an almost unlimited pool of able graduates who are more than happy to work for them.

GE, British Airways and American Express led the way, and the list of companies, which have followed them, grows every day.

Likewise in the software industry, the technology boom and the year-2000 bug problem meant that demand for programming skills far outstripped supply. British companies found it almost impossible to recruit and retain staff and had to pay exorbitant rates for the programmers they could find.

India offered a pool of extremely talented IT staff that would work for a fraction of the wages their UK counterpart demanded.

The fact of jobs moving to Asia is nothing new, of course. Britain's manufacturing industry declined steadily since the Second World War under the remorseless impact of low cost goods from overseas. In the 1980s, the loss of manufacturing jobs was justified to the British public as a painful but necessary part of the transition to a 'service' economy.

Dirty dangerous jobs mining coal or making tank gearboxes would be replaced with jobs in the burgeoning service sector. And service jobs, the theory went, would stay in this country. You could put a car or a shirt in a container and ship it across the world. But how could you do the same with a service?

All too easily, it turned out. The same call centres, as time revealed, that were being set up to bring jobs to the desolate mining towns and industrial cities of Wales, Scotland or the North of England or were now following the factories they replaced — heading offshore.

Naturally, this hasn't been allowed to happen without some opposition. Variation of the classic holiday t-shirt began to appear, bearing the slogan, "My job went to India and all I got was this lousy t-shirt".

Unsurprisingly, trade unions have spoken out against the trend for labour to head offshore to India.

After Abbey National sent 400 jobs from Warrington and Derby to Singapore, Linda Rolph, general secretary of the Abbey National Group Union complained to the press, "There is a stampede of jobs leaving the UK like this and the UK government seems unable to stop it."

Peter Woods, a forty-five-year-old IT consultant from Wanstead, in East London, believes that outsourcing in general has affected his business. "If you talk to individuals, they can't point to people who have taken their jobs away," he says. "But I have found that the gaps between jobs have got longer and longer and the rates have got lower and lower."

There are many reasons for the current hard times in the sector, he believes — 9/11, terrorist attacks, the fallout from the dot-com boom, and competition from overseas workers has affected his business.

"I think it has depressed rates," he says. "But not specifically India. If you look at Eastern Europe, they are even better positioned to compete than Indians are."

However, though the issue has caused real pain to many individuals and some local areas, it has never made much of an impact on the political agenda.

For many years now, the immigration question has been guaranteed to whip the right-wing British press into hysteria. It seems destined to become a massive issue in the forthcoming general election. But off-shoring has remained for most people a subject for the occasional wry cartoon or t-shirt gag. It has had nothing like the same impact on the political agenda.

Tony Blair was recently able to bat the question away with nonchalance: "Of course I feel desperately sorry for anyone whose job is at risk as a result of this change but that is the way the world is today. It may not be what people always want to hear but it is the truth. We have not tried to pretend to people we can stop what is happening in the global economy."

Of course, UK enjoys stubbornly low unemployment rates. Thus, far only 50,000 jobs have been off-shored, according to Amicus, the trade union that is most vocal in its opposition to off-shoring and that total is expected to rise to around 200,000 by 2008 — still a relatively low number in terms of the overall economy.

Nonetheless, the process of off shoring is still very much in its infancy. White-collar professionals can afford to be smug while t-shirt wearing programmers feel the sharp end of the global economy.

But there's no telling where the off-shorer's axe will fall next. Investment banks such as Bear Stearns and Lehman Brothers are already getting the more mundane research jobs done by bright graduates in India, who don't require the massive bonuses that London's bankers enjoy. Even journalists aren't safe — Reuters recently hired six reporters to cover US companies from Bangalore.

Reading headlines about this makes everyone nervous. It will be interesting to see if the public sector, which has grown considerably since the Labour party landslide of 1997, will also embrace outsourcing. That would be quite a shock — many civil servants put up with dull jobs and low wages because they expect cast iron job security.

Every company with large outsourcing or manufacturing requirements will have considered outsourcing on some level. But many companies decide against India in favour of staying in the UK or going somewhere closer like Eastern Europe.

Some cite time zones and distance as their reasons. Many find the bustle and pollution of large cities like New Delhi to be a deciding factor. They don't wish to visit these places themselves and fear they will have trouble asking colleagues to make regular visits.

Justifiably or not, India is not yet synonymous with quality. "I've certainly encountered that perception," says Mark Kobayashi-Hillary, an independent consultant who follows the Indian software business closely. But then this perception can change and is changing. "People see the pictures on TV, perhaps of the election, and you see cows and goats on the streets. People think how I get world-class software from a country like that. But I've taken people out there, and it's almost been like a religious conversion," he says.

The offshore IT industry has been quite proactive in counteracting this perception. Many Indian outsourcers were proactive in pursuing independent quality certifications such as the Capability Maturity Model and the ISO, in advance of many of their Western counterparts.

But there are plenty of stories of people who have received poor customer service from Indian call centres. It wasn't long ago that most account holders would know their local bank manager personally, and were used to calling their local branch. Many people don't like the service they get from call centres in the UK. So they're already tense and irritated when they phone up. So it's not surprising that people half a world away, speaking a second language, can't give them the experience they want.

In February Richard Pym, chief executive of the UK bank Alliance and Leicester said that his company had decided to keep its call centers in the UK for two reasons: "Firstly, because customers prefer it. Customers tell us they are transferring their business to us because of that. Secondly, for security reasons. The greater the geographical distance, the greater the security risk." US computer maker Dell's decision to close a call centre in India may not be the last. And Capital One's decision to terminate a contract after call centre workers gave out loans they weren't meant to highlights an issue that worries many offshorers — How can you ensure that tough data protection standards and other regulations are strictly observed in a call centre run 5,000 miles away by a separate company?

Whatever concerns some chief executives may have, it's clear that the tide is only flowing in one direction. The allure of highly skilled people who are willing to work hard for low wages will always force British companies to look abroad. Just as the flow of work abroad is inevitable, the backlash will come inevitably too. People who fear for their jobs will seek someone to blame.

Management consultancy McKinsey, claims that every dollar that goes to India returns as $1.14 to the home countries, through cheaper services to consumers, redeployment of staff to better paid jobs and added exports to India. This is analysis which should apply equally to the US and UK, McKinsey says.

It may be true, but that's cold comfort if yours is one of the jobs that goes. It's also cold comfort to people who feel that the services they're used to, from shops or banks to directory enquiries, are becoming harder and harder to reach, as companies cut costs. There will be a backlash, and it's likely to get worse. Ultimately, the long-standing cultural sympathy between the two countries may be a key factor in helping Britain to overcome the backlash, and try to maximise the potential benefits of the growth in the international service economy.

There have been several stories about Indian call centre workers being encouraged to watch English soap operas to help them empathise with their UK customers. Perhaps British managers should start taking Bollywood dance classes.

MANY INDIAS

THE CONTRASTS

One would imagine all in India is well if one closes this book here. The perception of India has changed, the global presence increasing and the media at home and outside is thrilled critically appreciating this large nation. True, but stopping here would be a half-truth. It would be an unfair conclusion besides being an inappropriate and incomplete definition of India.

After all, there is more to India and Indians than a growing economy, skilled IT professionals and entrepreneurship.

It is difficult to ignore the growing urban middle class, how their lifestyle has changed and how many more are now part of this segment. The growth of this class and its influence ties in with the advent of sectors such as advertising and retailing. The connection between them now is almost a circle which is not exactly vicious. The Indian advertising Indian has not merely assisted in creating consumerism but has lent to the positioning of a new Indian woman. At the same time, it has made retailing a relevant and an obvious by product as the demand and curiosity generated by advertising has to have a supply point. The advent of these industries and successes are contributors to Indian pride just as much as the change of perception of the nation and its people.

At the same time, there is abject poverty and an almost beleaguered farm sector. Levels of literacy are still very low. However, the electorate — most of who sit outside urban

India — is not asleep or completely tired of the lack of development in many areas — there is a surge and awareness that has possibly not been seen in the past. This is a change and the mix that exists and is part of the changing India.

Thomas L. Friedman in one of his many articles on India recently wrote that he visited a school that was "an hour's drive and ten centuries from Bangalore, India's Silicon Valley."[1] This remark defined the contrasts of India where even a short drive can take you to a different era or time zone. His article talks of a school of untouchables that most of urban modern India is not exposed to or hardly thinks of.

Certainly India is a country of contradictions and contrasts and plurality that only the Indian democracy knows. "India is often characterized as a country of contradictions. This idea is exemplified by the popular phrase that India accounts for close to a third of the world's software engineers and a quarter of the world's undernourished," suggests Goldman Sachs.[2]

It is only natural then that India has many Indias within it — some who are deprived of food and water and others who can easily afford a meal in London's most expensive hotel dressed in the best that France or Italy can offer when many Indians are totally unfamiliar with clothing.

While India ranks as the fourth largest economy in terms of purchasing power parity (as per some estimates), millions don't have jobs or money to spend. Roads in urban India may see the best of the automobile world, but cows, bullock carts and human rickshaws are not uncommon on the same streets.

The corporate and services sectors are beaming if not 'shining' but there are still millions of jobless as an estimated nine million hit the job market every year. About forty per cent of India's farmland goes without irrigation and yet the country is envied for its huge river network that should ideally have

---

[1] The IHT Online, Thomas L. Friedman: A Lesson in India, May 21, 2004.
[2] Goldman Sachs, India: Realizing BRICs Potential, April, 2004.

been the base for providing water to irrigate the country's huge farm sector. Mumbai, India's finance capital and arguably the most cosmopolitan city in the country, is home to Asia's largest slum dwelling. India's Reliance Industries has the largest shareholder base in the world and yet, hardly even three per cent of the nation's population are holders of stocks.

It is these differences, distinctions and contradictions that make India amazing, challenging, as mapping the Indian market is always a complex issue. India, to say the least, is not well connected even literally as roads are still to reach many remote parts of the nation and telephones are not a reality or of significance to many as they have a smaller presence than television sets — a fact that comes as a surprise to many as this is pretty much the opposite from the global trend. The advent of television is usually seen as positive in terms of information and entertainment but in a nation where jobs are hard to come by, the idiot box has frustrated many as it creates aspirations that cannot be fulfilled easily. Television may also be responsible for emphasizing the distinctions between the haves and have-nots and is being seen as one of the reasons that toppled the last government — a significant influence that the polity, advertisers and possibly programmers are aware of.

This part of the book attempts to cover key sections of India that reflect the metaphors of life in this large nation contrasting the weak and poor with the influential that are part of a 'progressive' and 'shining' India. There are four themes, that of the Indian electorate, the urban class and the darker side of the nation that is defined in the state of human resource development, the stagnation in the farm sector and unemployment.

It is important to point out that there are five write-ups related to the urban class. This is primarily since they have been part of the factors that have reclassified and redefined India being the beneficiaries of the economic reforms programme that are being seen as the foundation of a change. The urban Indian mind is intriguing and the influence of advertising is significant in not just influencing the way one lives, but also in creating a space for consumerism that has resulted in a retail-boom. Advertising has not just laid the seed for aspirations but has also leant to pride and nationalism besides giving urban Indians a new life while giving the much-maligned and ill-treated Indian woman a new place or stature in the growing new urban Indian cities.

This section starts off with the role of the advertising sector. And as you read on, it unfolds the many Indias that live together yet in isolation.

THE CREATIVE INDIAN

Santosh Desai

India Shining: catch-phrase or epitaph? The important thing is not whether this was a successful advertising campaign or not, but that what seems to be at the heart of the most surprising result in Indian electoral history is an advertising campaign. Surely, nothing demonstrates the new power of advertising in our consciousness than the discussion that surrounds these two words. In some ways, advertising has helped Market India believe that is also the voice of Electorate India, a belief with some tragic results for the ruling coalition.

How has advertising become so central in our sense of who we are? Large parts of India still lie outside the footprint of mass media advertising, so how has advertising arrogated so much importance to itself? The answer lies perhaps in the fact that advertising is the most visible, the most intrusive, and the most ubiquitous face of what has changed the most about India in the last decade or so.

Liberalization has allowed the Indian consumer access to a whole set of goodies that he only dreamed about earlier. Consumption is the new electricity that has thrilled middle class Urban India, which has energized a passive mass fearful till then of what tomorrow might suddenly decant on them. For most of urban India, the change that the reform process has unleashed is visible primarily through the window of consumption. Advertising is thus the most salient force that throbs with this new consumptive energy, being nothing but the chorus of mating cries shrieked by a whole host of new products in heat.

That alone makes advertising worth studying as a text from which to derive clues about what motivates a changing India.

By its very nature, advertising is a text that records our small everyday dreams. Advertising helps make our small lives big.

By magnifying the meaning resident in small everyday acts of gratification, impulse, anxiety and vanity, it helps construct the micro-narrative of our life.

By focusing on Life's Small Purposes, it is able to amplify our motivations about things that really drive us — it is perhaps the most honest account of who we are, what we dream of being, and what we would like the world to see us as.

Advertising recognizes us in a way that nothing else does — it finds us out only to exalt our smallness, our everyday humanness. Advertising helps us buy the symbolic magnification of ourselves; we are able to construct a fictional account of who we are based on the very real need of who we want to be. This makes the sum total of advertising that exists in the media at any given point in time a veritable river of dreams; we are able to understand the dominant drivers of any given era.

Advertising in pre-liberalisation India was really much more about products than about consumer desires. The print era made advertising a kind of privileged island inhabited by failed intellectuals. Some prominent exceptions like Liril apart, advertising was created for one's peers and created little impact on popular imagination. Cinema advertising depicted a vision of India so far removed from any reality that its role was really to build a dream-bubble around products than necessarily to speak to any consumer motivations. Campaigns for brands like Four Square (Live Life Kingsize), Nescafe (Come Alive with Nescafe) and Garden Vareli were some of the memorable ads created in this era. This was a time that a small elite consumed products and the primary pre-occupation of advertising was to ensure that it gave the brand a 'premium' image.

Most of the advertising was in English, and I remember many discussions about the possible image fallout if we also ran ads in the 'vernacular'.

The tone of advertising changed decisively with the advent of TV. Brands like Nirma, Rasna and Vimal infused a new energy, a throbbing vitality into the marketing discourse. Here were brands that pulsated, for the first time, with promises of *access* — to a world of consumption to which most of us had been denied entry. In their tonality too, these brands were brazen; there were no subtle puns, no esoteric allusions. Nirma made detergents available to Hema, Jaya, Lata and Sushma, Rasna ended our agonized denial of exotic squashes to the children in the house and Vimal seduced us with polyester-textured possibilities, a world far removed from ultramarine stained white shirts ironed by being put under mattresses.

In retrospect, it is easy to see how advertising, as a collective, and as part of the media at large, played its part in defrosting our restraint about the world of consumption. Products began to speak to underlying motivations, pleasure was gradually legitimized, the senses were privileged over cognition, habit gave way to the idea of personal choice and the past was increasingly made a monument to pay homage to rather than be led by.

This transition was made possible by a whole set of campaigns over the last decade. Let me describe the few that made a decisive impact.

Bajaj was the first brand that articulated the idea of Indian-ness, something that was tacitly understood to be a sort of skeleton rattling in the cupboards of the industry's consciousness till then. The *Hamara* Bajaj campaign, a stirring ode to our urban middle-classness was sought to convert frugality from being a desperate device to cope to being an essential part of our value system and in doing so began to free us from being bound by it. It allowed us to consume our Indian-ness; we were now conscious of our own impulses and hence no longer the prisoners we were to them.

We can trace the current strain of consumerism that we are experiencing to two brands, of which only one features advertising in a starring role. The Maruti 800 is the unlikely mother of Indian consumerism. The Maruti was the gift horse India gaped at the mouth of. Used as we were to the recalcitrant stinginess of the Ambassador and the Fiat, we were overwhelmed by the bounty that the Maruti showered on us.

The Maruti blurred fatally the line between Us and Them, those who drove cars and the rest who waited seven years for a Bajaj Chetak. The Maruti made us believe that we could escape the urban middle-class in our lifetime. The accessories that the car was showered with, the slogans it engendered (Papa says No Slogan); the musical horns it unleashed are all testimony to its crucial role in freeing up our consumption desires. The Maruti is its own ad — nothing that could be said about could better what it said about itself.

The other brand that broke through our consumption reserve was Pepsi. In many ways, the launch commercial, which shows a Pepsi bottle being coaxed rhythmically till it orgasmically bursts through the cap; is a fitting metaphor for the effect it had on the Indian consumer. Pepsi told us that it was all right for consumption to be frivolous; there really was nothing official about it.

A brand that really set the sexual cat among the moral pigeons was Kama Sutra. The idea of contraception in India was always part of the State's Grand Plan to keep population under control. The condom was part thus of every citizen's duty to build a prosperous India. The brand name Nirodh, which evokes images of awkward abstinence, was part of this strategy. Kama Sutra did the unthinkable; it associated the condom with the act of sex and promoted the idea of pleasure rather than restraint.

Another kind of loosening was ushered in by another frivolous category — potato chips. The earliest salvo was fired

by a brand that no longer exists in any meaningful way —
Binnie's. The *Humko* Binnie's *Mangta* (I want Binnie's)
campaign was, however, a highly influential one, being virtually
the first campaign that used street language. *Humko* Binnie's
Mangta, hardly an advertising classic in retrospect, however,
triggered a fundamental change in the kind of advertising that
was being created in India. The emphasis shifted from the seller
to the buyer; advertising began to be created in a language she
could respond to.

This meant a big power shift within the industry — the
anglicized South Bombay set, which had dominated the
industry from the outset started becoming irrelevant.
Advertising began to be created in the local language and began
to look for stories from everyday life.

The move towards the local was strengthened by the
renewed belief in the resilience of the Indian way to life in spite
of being under attack from Western skies. A campaign that
captured this pride came from an unlikely source — Channel
V. Entrusted with the task of making Indian youth a part of the
global collective, the brand found instead that its strongest
connection with the consumer lay in re-affirming the local-ness
of Indian youth. We are Like This Only is an affectionate
affirmation of our often bewilderingly idiosyncratic ways.

Over the last five years, the Indianisation of Indian
advertising is perhaps the single most perceptible change that
can be discerned by an observer. As the consumption energies
of more and more people are being released, advertising is
casting its net ever wider. The *Thanda Matlab* (Cold means)
Coca Cola campaign is perhaps the pinnacle of this trend; it
inverts completely the traditional synthetic images associated
with aerated soft drinks.

Advertising has also documented the changing aspirations
of the woman in many different ways. The housewife is no
longer the tense hand-maiden to everyone else's expectations,
but someone who is in full control of her domain. The Surf
campaign over time reveals the evolution in the housewife's

sense of control over her own domain. The pre-liberalisation Lalita*ji* campaign featured the protagonist aggressively responding to a challenging male voice off-screen. Lalita*ji* demolished all doubts about her good sense being posed by her male inquisitor one by one till she finally won his approval.

The post-liberalisation *Dhoondte Reh Jaaoge* (You'll keep finding) campaign features a woman with much greater natural authority over her domain — when her husband dares challenge her wisdom; he is laughed off almost contemptuously. The housewife's fundamental role hasn't changed; but her control over it has. The advertising mirrors the change in the woman's self image — today she, the consumption protagonist, is vested with the authority to make most decisions about what household products to consume. She has also moved from being a performer to being a participant in the construction of joy for the family. Depictions of the mother as friend, prankster and cheerleader all rolled into one are common today. Her being continues to be described by her many roles, but is no longer contained by them.

Two other campaigns that helped expand the boundaries for representations of women in advertising have been the Cadbury's Dairy Milk and the Ericsson phone campaigns. The former encapsulated in an iconic image of a girl celebrating with abandon at a cricket match, the unexpressed desires of many women. The Ericsson campaign had the woman in icy control, imperiously oblivious to the pathetic fantasies that men seem to entertain.

The idea of female beauty has undergone a significant change. Fuelled by the beauty pageant successes we saw a few years ago, the notion of beauty has changed from being a natural blessing to being a manufacturable utility. The ideas of *changing* one's destiny, of *reversing* time, of *erasing* blemishes, of *constructing* a desired persona are all manifestations of the new feeling that how you look is critical but that it lies within your control.

The other big change we have seen in Indian advertising has been the growing use of celebrities by more and more brands. Celebrities by virtue of being man-made Gods, help validate the consumption dream. In the Indian context, the idea of social mobility gets dramatically re-inforced by the examples set by celebrities. Advertising, at its heart, promises magical transformations; nothing exemplifies these better than celebrities.

The story of how advertising has impacted India's move towards a market economy would be incomplete without acknowledging the central role played by television in bringing about this change.

Unlike print, which operates through the mind and is hence disseminated down the axis of education, with those with greater educational resources being privy to more, television operates through the senses and is more democratic in its appeal. Anyone who can afford a TV can access all it has to offer. TV has helped unleash a new energy, a new confidence in the Indian urban middle class. The TV legitimizes personal desire, with the remote control being a metaphor for having the things you want, when you want them. The transience of the TV image makes experience more important than reflection and converts everything to its surface. Television makes the world a spectacle manufactured for our consumption — it is market capitalism's foundation.

What Indian advertising has done is really to take the logic implicit in television forward — it has over the last decade helped democratize aspirations, given consumers a greater sense of control over their own personal destiny, it has made the present a more attractive place to live in than the past and it has helped legitimize living through the senses.

Advertising has played a role in constructing among the urban middle class a sense of a shiny new self. It has done so without threatening the sense of continuity in the Indian way of life. Advertising has helped the urban middle class Indian feel good about herself; the Indian voter is another story.

The next logical move after advertising is not just getting products on to the shelves. The issue is, and has been, to make the availability more accessible and if possible, more attractive. And this, in the Indian context, did not necessarily mean just packaging, it meant getting better shelves and stores that could relate to the consumer and the product. While this is a gradual change, it is happening and the improved stores or the mall culture taking up a huge bit of Gurgaon is an indication of the advancement and of things to come.

The pace of change over the past year or so has been so great if not aggressive that Gurgaon, is being touted as the possible retail capital of Asia! Apparently, now this sector is being recognized far more than the mere corner store (that has worked well and looks better than ever). The transition and the possibilities in the future explain why foreign investors have been pressing successive governments to open up the retail space to foreign direct investment (FDJ).

The following chapter gives you a glimpse into the complex Indian retail sector including the growing interest in the rural and tribal belts of the country. It also brings to fore the size of the consuming class and the general trends.

CONSUMING THE RETAIL BOOM

Rumy M. Narayan

It is there to be seen. There is a clear shift towards aggressive and vibrant consumption patterns both in the urban as well as non-urban areas, preparing the ground for a full-scale retail revolution. The proliferation of newer products and more extensive product categories into these markets will entail more sophisticated supply systems as well as retail environments and such pressures would mount as the Indian consumers start to discern.

We are already witnessing a steady development in organized retail activity in urban India. Several players are getting into the retail business in India to introduce new formats like malls, supermarkets, discount stores, departmental stores and even changing the traditional looks of bookstores, chemist shops, and furnishing stores.

But as this section of the book points out, India is a place of bizarre contrasts. So while we gloss over the huge malls and the improved stores in terms of look and feel, we must note that formats fall under the organized retail category and still forms a minuscule part of the total retail trade in India. The total retail market in India is estimated to be over US $240 billion, of which the organized segment with formats like multi brand stores, malls, super stores, franchise agreements and company owned single brand stores, is currently estimated to be only two per cent of the total retail sales in the country.

Retailing employs more than twenty million people, but the share of employment remains far below the true potential. The value added at retailing is quite low due to huge losses resulting from disorganized industry and the presence of a long chain of middlemen.

There are nearly twelve million retail outlets in the country, which gives India the distinction of having the highest number of retail outlets as a percentage of population in the world. But retail space at a mere two square feet per capita drags it down to the bottom of the list. After all India's retail space is known more for its corner stores than anything else.

But then, India is an evolving market and the numbers are bound to change. Over the past decade, the shift towards organized formats in retailing has been impressive and the last year or so has marked a hyped presence of the mall culture. Industry watchers point out that organized retail in India will grow at least by thirty per cent by 2005.

Retailers in India, be it Shoppers' Stop or Pantaloon have learnt the dynamics of the Indian market place through trial and error and have worked out their own brand of strategy based on their understanding of the markets they operate in. Some like ITC are looking at tapping their existing distribution networks to enter organized retail not just in urban areas but also in rural areas. For instance, ITC is looking at selling a whole host of products through its e-choupal (an online information service meant for farmers) networks. Incidentally, the e-choupal initiative was started by ITC to add value and develop its agricultural business.

Similarly, when promoters of the malls in Gurgaon (a fast developing suburb of New Delhi) found that there are not enough brands to occupy space in their swanky developments, they devised a way to lure popular and established Delhi-based retail stores and restaurants to open up branches in the malls. This is now a trend among old time retailers even from smaller towns and cities. But as the market matures and becomes more complex and organized retail captures a larger share of the market, retailers will find it difficult to manage growth and also stay relevant in the market place.

The reason for this lies in the complex nature of the Indian market. India is going through an important transformation that is very vibrant as well as chaotic. Also, globalization has meant that such transitions are not happening over fifty years but within a space of four to eight years. In order to capture these changes and remain relevant to the different bands of consumers, product marketers are constantly trying to categorize them in terms of age, income levels, gender and lifestyles.

Before going further, let's look at some statistics about the consumer so as to have a direct bearing on the industry both on the demand as well as the supply side. This data also throws light on how and why retail is slowly moving towards organized forms.

The total population of India is 1.04 billion, of this number currently, about fifty per cent are below the age of forty-five and it is estimated that by 2006, about 61.9 per cent of the population will be between the age of fifteen to fifteen years, that is, the total productive population[1].

Per capita income for the urban middle class has been and continues to clock an impressive growth, giving a large fillip to demand for various products. According to consulting firm KSA-Technopak's annual Consumer Outlook 2003 survey conducted across twenty cities, the discretionary income for the top consuming class is between Rs 55,000-60,000. Significantly, this excludes expenditure on fuel, education, health, rent and utilities.

More statistics here but they are relevant.

Of this income, the Indian tends to spend as much as forty per cent on food and grocery (spending on food remains high

---

[1] Statistical Outline of India 2002-2003.

but this share is steadily declining, this points to the fact that the market is fast maturing and as income levels go up, consumption of so-called 'luxury' products will go up).

Eating out is in and a sure positive for the food retail business as twelve per cent of the spending pie goes at restaurants and cafes. Then seven to eight per cent is spent on apparel, two per cent on footwear and six to seven per cent on personal care. In 2003, corporate salaries in India grew at over ten per cent, faster than most of the developed economies and the study indicated that discretionary spending has risen by fifteen per cent during the same period.

And if it was thought that India was still very, very nascent, the survey suggests that India may not have matured but it is not all that nascent. It was found that there were three evolving customer categories, technology babies, between the ages eight to nineteen years, the impatient aspirers (twenty to twenty-five years) and the balance seekers (twenty-six to fifty years).

The first category of consumers are extremely tech-savvy and have a weakness for gadgets, this segment splurges on books, music, mobile phones, eating out, apparel and footwear.

The second category of 'impatient aspirers', actively look for creativity and customization in their consumption targets. This category of consumers is typically independent, indulgent and career-driven followed by the 'balance seekers', who are the sophisticated, cautious and sober consumers and whose main concern is convenience. This category of consumers also exhibit a great deal of fondness for gadgets but it is more due to their being status conscious than real interest in such gizmos.

Most consumer surveys show that there is a rapid evolution from basic consumption products to luxuries and a credit-friendly system is spurring more and more urban Indians to make this transition. The urban consumer is spending a large part of its income on consumer durables, music, homes and entertainment.

This spending orgy is both reflected and celebrated in the media and with the media making swift and determined inroads into the rural innards of India, rural India is also waking up to the consumer culture and are showing clear signs of aspirations. This need or desire among the rural part of the country comes at a time when the market players have realized the need to move on and increase their spread.

What has been noted is that with urban markets getting saturated for basic consumption products and the markets showing an increased trend towards replacing and upgrading products, marketers are making a beeline for the rural markets. And with good reason: while the urban markets are stabilizing at growth levels of seven to ten per cent, the rural markets are clocking a robust growth rate of twenty-five per cent annually[2]. Durable manufacturers such as LG, Samsung, Onida and others expect at least sixty-five to seventy per cent of their total sales in terms of volumes to come from smaller markets.

As marketers make inroads into these markets, the media has also followed with customized offerings, first to small towns and now slowly into rural areas in the form of local language newspapers and TV channels. These local language media offerings are carefully designed to match the sensibilities of the small towns they cater to and at the same time, create aspirations for its users in a way that is parallel to their urban counterparts. The main effort here is interactive programming where camera teams visit the viewer's homes and create a game around such activities. The television channel builds goodwill and the sponsor gets more mileage.

Such strategies are working in these parts of India even though these aspirations are not manifested in the same way as the urban consumer they are reflected in lifestyle changes among the rural and tribal belts in India.

---

[2] *Business Standard*, Switching on in rural India by Arti Sharma, April 3, 2004.

The Delhi School of Economics' Department of Developmental Economics has been carrying out extensive research in the tribal areas of Madhya Pradesh for quite some time. The key points worth highlighting from this research project are changes in consumption patterns in these tribal areas, dissatisfaction with the government-provided education system, greater awareness of what is happening in the world outside and the aspiration to be part of this great consumer boom. Supriya Singh, one of the researchers on the ground points out how the food habits of the tribals are slowly changing. In Jhabua, where she did extensive research among the trials she saw how products alien to their culture like milk and carbonated soft drinks (CSD) are slowly creeping in.

During the weekly bazaars, young people prefer to drink milk-based products like *lassi* or if they really want to flaunt their status a bottle of CSD is the way to go. She also noticed that with roads and communication links getting better, there is a great deal of dissatisfaction among the tribals about their way of life.

These tribal communities, for whom the barter system was a way of life, are increasingly becoming conscious of the importance of money. She says that money has become so important for these tribals that many have stopped making traditional patterns in their handicrafts, most of their handicrafts are now influenced by what the market outside is looking for. Now the traditional patterns are crafted only for their own use.

For sure there is a huge market out there. A National Council of Applied Economic Research (NCAER) survey reveals that, of all middle-income households — those with a total annual income of between Rs. 35,000 and Rs. 140,000 — two-thirds are in the rural areas. Of the 60 million high-income households — those with annual incomes above Rs. 140,000 — one-third live in the countryside. It also predicts that ownership of durables will go up from 835 million in 2001-02 to 1.4 billion by 2006-07.

But understanding this market is not necessarily all that easy. This explains why for instance, advertising agency RK Swamy BBDO recently launched a guide to effective market planning for urban India. The guide covers 784 towns in 21 states and three union territories with populations over 50,000. The chief aim of this guide is to provide well-rounded information on a town's market potential.

Traditionally marketers tend to think that affordability is the first key ingredient of market potential but the guide reveals that affordability by itself may not translate into purchase. Ownership of consumer durables and FMCG (fast-moving consumer goods) usage are indicators of the extent to which a town is spending. Media awareness is important too, as it provides information on what to buy and where. The guide also looked at whether the town has the infrastructure to spur consumption. Indications of market support were arrived at by studying figures of per capita employment in trade, transport and bank credit to these sectors. Added to the check list to gauge a market were per capita income, per capita bank deposit, proportionate affluent households with monthly income greater than Rs 10,000, ownership of consumer durables, consumption of FMCG, print media readership, television viewership, other mass media awareness and usage.

The need to carry out such studies emphasizes the size and the need to penetrate markets outside the typical metropolitan cities of the country. What is clear is that India has a huge market and now with the advent of television, advertising, Indian-specific programming and a better understanding among consumers even in rural spaces, it can be realized more easily than before. For a developing and populous country like India, encouraging consumption is one of the best ways to create employment for the masses. Every additional TV sold creates a job not just in manufacturing and retail level but also in the after-sales service markets. The boom in consumption has already created hundreds of jobs in organized retail and as organized retail captures a larger share of the market, hundreds of more jobs will be created.

If there are concerns, they are related to habits of consumers in that whether they are as yet in the know of the harmful effects of such large-scale consumption on the environment. India has traditionally been a society where recycling has played an important role, but the new consumer culture has been encouraging the 'use and throw' attitude within the burgeoning consuming class. Will Indian consumers for example, raise a voice against environmentally unfriendly practices? Maybe.

It is possible that an aware Indian consumer would force a McDonald's to team up with an environmental agency like its parent did in the US to look at ways of reducing packaging and greater use of recycled materials. Such awareness could set off a trend just like the Indian shopper realized the difference between a discount sale in developed retail markets such as the US, Malaysia, Dubai or Thailand. A discount sale of ten to twenty per cent is hardly a sale for an Indian anymore but a discount is attractive when the cut in price is 'real' enough.

For sure, the market thought of in the early 1990s is now here to be reached. If there is any caution, it is the complexity. But then Indian ingenuity is something that can help in penetration the huge consumer base that the nation offers.

A PERSPECTIVE TO THE TRENDY
URBAN INDIAN

Even as the retail boom took place, the lifestyle of the urban Indian started changing and the pace over the last couple of years has been pretty dramatic. Maybe the change was simultaneous and complimentary. This seems more likely given that the lifestyle, particularly of the urban upper middle class that spends a lot, has a lot do with the creation of niche retail spaces be it food, apparels or anything else for that matter. The rise in sale of luxury vehicles is an indication of the kind of salaries and surplus cash that the new urban Indian has.

Foreign tourists visiting India often get shocked at the lifestyle of the affluent class or even the upper middle and not as rich class particularly in cities such as Mumbai and New Delhi. They wonder how the Indians have acquired such tastes and 'style', if one may call it.

There could be a story or reason for this change — good or bad. The presence of Indians as tourists across the globe is on the rise. According to a report,[1] there would be six million Indians travelling overseas during 2004, of which about 1.5 million would be leisure travellers. This figure could 'swell to 50 million by 2020.' What is significant is that the Indian

---

[1] *Sunday Times of India*, New Delhi, June 6, 2004, 'Going Places Club Class' by Jug Suraiya.

spends well if not big and a significant bit goes on food, shopping, drinking and 'generally having a blast'.

More importantly, like many other studies, this report points out, "According to the Swiss, Indians spend between US $350 and US $ 450 a day." This is second to the Japanese, it adds.

How important is this to the urban Indians lifestyle? A lot.

Such holidays and exposure even in areas such as Southeast Asia, (among the new destinations that interests Indians of late) has resulted in the opening up of the Indian mind to new tastes and flavours besides a different lifestyle. While television has done its bit, the reality of experiences from travelling across the shores, is more powerful in making an impact. It is not an invasion of foreign cultures but the acquiring of the same and at times an adaptation of it in an Indian way. Dheeraj Arora, the twenty-nine-year-old running New Delhi's Shalom says that the urban Indian is now in a position to compare the food served at a restaurant in the Capital with what they ate, say somewhere in Europe. This makes them more demanding and Indian eateries more conscious of specific cuisines, he added.

To cater to such needs, the Indian retail space has made way for food retail outlets such as Olive or Shalom, Mantra or Forum, Indigo or Moshe's Oliva — the count is countless. The Fashion Bar is yet another example of the new lifestyle and so is Mocha. And you can be sure, a Shalom, Olives or a Mocha would hardly have a table vacant on any given day of the week.

While travelling is one reason for the prolific turnover in the number of eateries and variety in cuisine, the pressures of the new work culture is another reason for the changing face of Indian cities. With an increasing number of working couples and the disintegration of joint families, the Indian is slowly but surely preferring to eat out and then return home after a hard day's work. Besides, this is now being seen as a source for unwinding.

Spending on oneself is also not a no-no anymore. The emergence of fashion in the Indian urban mind plays to this new fancy and has resulted in an emphasis on designer outlets of the Rohit Bals, and Manish Aroras, and shows such as the Lakme India Fashion Week. In fact, India has its own fashion television channel, Trendz (part of the Zee Group). And FTV has more Indian programming than before.

The point is that the Indian urban lifestyle — at least a section — is now inching closer to the West. The significance of art and music is on the rise and so is the space for theatre. While some of the interest is purely a fad, there are many who actually appreciate and know.

Get a look into the new urban Indian lifestyle and how the market has moved and reshaped itself.

LIFE IN THE NEW URBAN MIDDLE

Malavika Sangghvi

O n a sultry day in April 2004, Tommy Hilfiger, the iconic American casual clothing czar was ensconced in a suite at the Oberoi hotel in Mumbai, perspiring elegantly into his pinstripes and giving interviews as if they were going out of style. Though the pitch changed with every new hack, the theme was consistent: Tommy and his brand of sports-inspired street chic is coming to India to make hay while the Indian sun was shining.

Ever since the early 1990s when the government began liberalizing the economy and services industries such as banking, insurance, and healthcare and IT were booming, Indian markets began to be an attractive proposition for foreign companies, particularly those catering to the needs of the younger Indian.

More than forty-five per cent of Indians are under twenty, and KSA Technopak, a consulting firm estimates that young people in India command US $10.5 billion in spending power. And with the buying muscle in this section rising by about twelve per cent a year, more than twice the pace of the growth of the economy in this country, Hilfiger and others like him know they are on to a very good thing indeed. India is the world's second most populous nation and home to the world's largest urban middle-class (the size of the American population at last count.)

The NCAER, in one of its surveys says that the category of 'very rich' in India has also expanded from 2.5 million people in 1990 to roughly 33 million in 2000 which is roughly the population of Argentina. And when you take in to consideration that the US Department of Commerce ranks India as one of the ten largest emerging markets in the world, the fast-changing landscape of India's 200 cities, the stomping grounds for populations of over 100,000 citizens with an appetite for telephones, cars, television sets, clothes, refrigerators, burgers pizzas, sneakers and yes, Hilfiger jeans, you can see why India is an attractive story on the world map.

And who would have thought that things were so very different not so long ago.

In the 'Bad Old Days', (as I would like to call it, having seen India then and now) before the Indian economy got sexy and software was a badly washed pajama suit, there are those amongst us, who survived, and lived to tell the tale.

Indians drove in one or the other of the very old and weird make of cars that were available: the Fiat and the Ambassador.

Clothes had to be ordered from the tailor down the road, copied from well-leafed and frayed ancient fashion magazines procured from abroad; there was only one TV channel to view and it was black and white and government-run, movies were watched in decrepit rat-infested cinema halls and travelling Indians stuffed their bags with vinyl analog records, jeans, Scotch, chocolates, perfumes and even underwear, in fact, whatever they could lay their hands on from the fancy malls of developed nations before returning home, as if these items were contraband (and according to Indian Custom rules, they most likely were).

There were no malls, no restaurants barring a few in five star hotels, no night life to speak of and very little entertainment.

How different to today where the Indian consumer has a galaxy of Japanese and Korean cars to choose from. (In Communist run Calcutta or Kolkata, no less, newly registered cars are flooding the streets at a rate of 3,000 a month.)

Today, there are over 400 major supermarkets in India. Citibank, the largest issuer of credit cards in India has a subscriber base of 1.4 million. India has over eighteen million mobile-phone users. McDonalds has forty-eight stores in India, sixty per cent of them built in the past eighteen months. (The outlets see up to 3,000 customers a day, placing the units in the company's top ten per cent with expected sales to grow forty per cent annually in the coming years.) Motorola says sales of its mobile phones in India increased 200 per cent in the first six months over the same period last year.

According to KSA Technopak, Indians spent fifty-five per cent more money eating out in 2002 than the year before. India is the world's largest market for blenders and the second largest for scooters. In the past two years, the number of new credit cards issued has jumped twenty-five per cent annually and new mortgage thirty-five per cent. Sales of Reebok footwear are growing thrity per cent a year. Mumbai-based Inox Leisure opened its first two multiplexes over the past year and is investing US $50 million to build 11 more, with as many as 6 screens by mid 2005. In 1975, only one million Indians were investors in the stock market. In 2000, that figure grew to nineteen million.

Welcome to the new urban India, with its glitzy restaurants shopping malls, glass and chrome IT hubs, health-clubs, fast-food joints, multiplexes, coffee-bars luxury housing complexes and Page Three culture.

Meet the new wine-swilling, sneaker-wearing, golf-playing urban Indian, clutching his Japanese made camera-mobile phone, jetting to work in a private-owned airline, bidding for consumer goods on the internet with his credit card, watching movies in multiplexes at the same time as his counterpart abroad, and feeling very, very pleased with himself indeed.

In the new scenario, pop stars from abroad regularly drop in to croon to the crowds, beauty contests and film award ceremonies break out like a rash and daily soap operas command the eyeballs of the populace. Young people take out loans to buy houses, cars, furniture, and holiday tickets. There is a brisk business in imported alcohol, gadgets and gizmos and ready-to wear apparel. Indians are travelling abroad more, buying more consumer durables and spending on lifestyle and entertainment like never before.

And to think none of this would have been possible if not for a case of some fortunate ineptness: busy with applying tight control on Indian industry in a heavily regulated economy the government plain forgot to interfere with software exporters in the late 1980s. The fortuitous oversight resulted in some extraordinary growth in this unregulated sector. Soon India, and in particular the southern city of Bangalore became one of the top ten software producing cities in the world, home to over 300 software companies and 150 high-tech multinationals prompting Bill Gates to predict that India is likely to be the next software super power.

This data and constant reference to the IT sector may seem a bit away from this section but it is relevant.

Bangalore's software exports soared from US $50 million to US $ 6.3 billion in 10 years. Accounting for 11.5 per cent of India's total exports it became India's fastest growing most Anglicized city with the largest population of middle class, and the world's premier supplier of skilled software engineers. This fillip to her sluggish economy had a ripple effect. IT jobs were created, salaries were brought more in line with world economies and a new consuming class was created.

Add to this the advent of the outsourcing business that came along when the world discovered that India has the second largest pool of English speaking populace after America and are cheaper in terms of cost compared to their counterparts in the US. This meant better money in the hands of the young, a huge number that were just out of college waiting to earn and spend. By 2000, more than 200 of the Fortune 1000 companies were outsourcing their requirements to India. From Bombay to Bangalore and Chennai to Chittagong, the best jobs in town were hunting for young people who spoke a reasonable smattering of English and who could be trained to man calls from Manhattan and Madrid. Graduates who once got salaries of Rs 5,000 to Rs 9,000 a month were now earning Rs 18,000 to 30,000.

Significantly, these young people unlike the older veterans of the IT industry, its engineers and scientists, did not carry the baggage of Mahatma Gandhi-inspired asceticism and consumer denial.

They were young, brash, hungry and ready to go. They didn't believe in saving, they lived for the moment, and their energy needs demands and dreams shaped Indian cities in to the consumer Valhallas that they are.

Their contribution to the economy has made consumer spending grow at an average of twelve per cent a year over the past decade. Five years ago, the average age of a Citibank mortgage holder was forty-one, now it is twenty-eight. Wipro Spectramind had only 200 employees at the end of 2000, today it has close to 10,000. The NASSCOM expects that one million people will be working in call centers and other back office operations in India by 2008, up from 1,60,000. And with the continued growth of the BPO and IT sector and a growth rate of a healthy seven per cent, there seems to be every indication that things can only get better.

According to the NCAER, the 'consuming class' (people reported to have an annual income between US $1300 and US $6,000 and who owned a TV, a cassette recorder, pressure cooker, ceiling fan, bicycle and wristwatch) is expected to triple in 10 years reaching 450 million people by 2010. India's urban middle class is expected to grow to 445 million by 2006, and the number of people living in households that earn at least US $1,800 annually — considered the minimum for middle class households — has increased 17 per cent in just the past three years to more than 700 million. At this level people can purchase two wheelers TVs and refrigerators. This segment is expected to rise an additional twenty-four per cent by 2007.

A study by property consultants Knight Frank shows that India will have about fifty-five new shopping malls by 2005. About 100 multiplexes are in the pipeline nationally. The NCAER estimates that the consuming class (annual income of Rs 45,000 to Rs 2,15,000) will be 75 million households in 2006. Goldman Sachs has predicted that India will become the world's largest economy by 2050.

For sure, there will be even more glass chrome and brick baroque palaces with Corinthian pillars and marble domes to house its rising new middle class aspirations. More bowling alleys and TV soaps like *Friends* to watch on the box, more fast food joints and more supermarkets selling international packaged goods. And then real estate prices in Bombay and Delhi, pegged at nearly the highest in the world today, will finally be justified, when these cities evolve in to some of the most modern and user-friendly in the world.

For those of us who have seen the transition, survived the Bad Old Days and lived to tell the tale, this will be reward enough.

Far from the cosmetics of the urban rich is the permanent ink that an Election Commission-appointed official smears on the index finger of a voter. This mark is meant to make sure that a voter does not return to cast a bogus vote. This norm is of little importance to the rich and the upper middle class of urban India who prefer to stay home rather than exercise their franchise.

It is those who are at the end of the social demographic line who still believe in exercising their franchise. For many, voting is their only way to express their satisfaction or frustration in a government, besides bestowing hope in leaders they vote for. And the past few elections has seen a marked change in the way the voter behaves. Patterns are not predictable and the voter seems to be evolving in a manner that reveals a new thinking of the Indian people and also the risks that any political party runs in India. The following several hundred words will take you through the nuances of the Indian electorate in the light of the political ground realities.

THE ELECTORATE AND ELECTORAL WISDOM

R. Shankar

T he Atal Bihari Vajpayee government that had been voted out has the distinction of being the first non-Congress government and also the first coalition to complete its term in office. While this fact has got the attention it deserves, the media and the chatteratti have been so consumed by the hype about the persona of Vajpayee that it is automatically put down to his acceptability to all constituents of the National Democratic Alliance (NDA) and his skills in managing a coalition.

These are obviously important factors in ensuring that the NDA government lasted, but to regard them as the sole factors or even the most crucial ones is to miss a more generalised trend. What has passed unnoticed in the process is the evidence that recent coalitions in New Delhi have tended to be more cohesive than earlier ones. The last Vajpayee government is the most obvious illustration of the point, but by no means the only one.

The two United Front governments of 1996 and 1997 for instance, had been brought down by the Congress. Yet, on neither occasion did the UF itself crack up. This was in sharp contrast to the experience of earlier coalitions.

In 1979, for example, the Janata Party government of Morarji Desai was brought down because it fell apart under the weight of its internal contradictions. The Congress did fish in troubled waters by supporting Charan Singh's bid to become prime minister, but the waters were troubled by the constituents of the Janata parivar themselves. Similarly, V.P. Singh's Janata Dal government fell because of differences between the Janata Dal and the BJP, one of its key allies. Again the Congress was more than willing to help the process of the breakdown, but what is more significant is the fact that — as in 1979 — a faction of the ruling party itself was quick to desert the sinking ship and play ball with the Congress. Seen in that context, the fact that the UF hung together through the fall of two governments was remarkable indeed and the first sign of the maturing of coalition politics in India.

The manner in which the Vajpayee government of 1998 was brought down might suggest that it is facile to see the UF's cohesion as the beginning of a trend. However, even on that occasion, there was a clear difference from the past. First, the government almost survived the withdrawal of support by its largest ally, the All India Anna Dravida Munnetra Kazhagam, failing to win the vote of confidence by a solitary vote. Most of the ruling coalition, thus, hung together even when the government's survival was in question. More importantly, the coalition more or less held firm even after the fall of the government, which is why the Congress' attempt to form an alternate government came a cropper.

Perhaps even more interesting than these signs of an increasing maturity in the manner in which political parties deal with coalitions is the evidence that the ordinary Indian voter has got to grips with the rules of the new game and is willing to give it a fair shot.

Consider the manner in which the electorate responded to the fall of coalition governments in the past and how that seems to have changed of late. In the general elections of 1980, which followed the collapse of the Janata Party experiment, the Congress won at a canter, the scattered remains of the ruling party being reduced to also-rans. Again, after the Janata Dal lost power in 1990, the electorate that had only a year-and-a-half earlier brought it to power with the support of the Left and the BJP rejected it conclusively in the 1991 general elections. The Congress, for a change, did not get a majority on its own, but again a ruling party had been severely punished for failing to survive its full term.

The electorate was clearly till this stage enamoured of the notion of 'stability' and still equated the government's ability to last a full term with the concept of stability.

An interesting pattern thus far had been the fact that the electorate seemed to hold the ruling party responsible for the instability of the government. Supporting parties, it seemed to be saying, were free to change their mind, the onus of keeping the ship afloat lay with those at the helm. Thus, though the Congress helped destabilize the Janata Party government in the late seventies and Chandrashekhar's government in 1991, the party was not punished by the electorate. Nor was the BJP for withdrawing support from the V.P. Singh government and hence bringing about its premature demise. On the contrary, in each of these cases while the party running the government had to bite the dust in the subsequent elections, the party responsible for destabilizing the government actually did better than it had in the previous elections.

The 1998 elections marked a break from this pattern. Some of the constituents of the United Front, most noticeably the Janata Dal, paid the price for their inability to keep the government going for its full term. But others, like the Telugu Desam Party (TDP), were certainly not punished by the electorate. On the contrary, the TDP won more seats in Parliament than ever before. Also, if there was some dissatisfaction with a coalition government falling much too soon once again, the anger rubbed off on the Congress too this time. Unlike in the past, the Congress tally in the Lok Sabha also declined. Here then, was some evidence of the average voter developing a more nuanced understanding of the nature of coalitions than in the past.

The 2004 elections provide evidence of the electorate becoming even more sophisticated. One overarching feature has been the refusal by the electorate to be taken in by media and official hype. The India Shining campaign was launched by the government, but taken up enthusiastically and unquestioningly by the mainstream media. With more than a month to go for polling date, the media had already pronounced its verdict — the NDA would romp home to victory, the 'Atal factor' would prove decisive. This, we were told, was the first government to be facing an election without an anti-incumbency disadvantage. In fact, there was if anything a pro-incumbency sentiment overriding all else in the election campaign.

It is hardly worth pointing out today how embarrassingly off the mark such analysis was.

What is worth pointing out is that the electorate, unlike the media, proved adept at discounting the hype. This election, we were told was to be about 'bijli, sadak, pani' (electricity, roads and water). The India Shining campaign was clearly aimed at suggesting that on these counts, the NDA had delivered. The voters seem to have agreed that bread and butter issues ought to be important in determining electoral outcomes, but decided to judge performance based on their lived experience rather than on media hype. This, of course, is not to suggest that factors like caste and community became irrelevant or even unimportant in the fourteenth general elections of the nation. Quite possibly, they remained the single most important factors.

However, the relative importance of more 'real' issues has arguably increased.

In this context, it is also worth questioning the assumption that 'identity politics' is necessarily in contradiction with politics based on issues. Arguably a more correct reading would be that identity politics builds on the disenchantment based on very real factors of specific groups and communities, but is not restricted to redressing those grievances. It would also help our understanding of electoral and political behaviour if we were to concede that self-respect is as real an issue as roads or power.

To return to the evidence on the growing maturity of the Indian voter in dealing with coalition politics, the most striking evidence in these elections came from the states of Uttar Pradesh and West Bengal. In both cases, the choice before the voters was between the NDA, the Congress and parties or fronts allied with neither the BJP nor the Congress. Interestingly, in both cases, the NDA and the Congress did badly, the others did extremely well.

Very clearly, the mere stability of governments is not something the electorate is any longer worked up about for its own sake in quite the same manner as it used to be in the past. Remember that after exit polls started projecting a hung Parliament as a possibility, the BJP completely switched tack and started focusing on stability as its main campaign plank. It is in this context that the results in the states that polled in the last phases on May 10 become particularly interesting. Of the 182 seats that polled on that day, the BJP won less than 30 seats, the Congress just over 40. The vast majority of the seats in the last phases, therefore, voted for other parties, even if about thirty of these were allies of the Congress or the BJP.

The electorate of UP knew fully well that rejecting both the BJP and the Congress and increasing the Samajwadi Party's tally could lead to a hung Parliament and very unstable coalitions. It does not seem to have regarded that as a scenario too terrible to contemplate. It is another matter that despite the SP getting its highest tally ever in the Lok Sabha, it does not quite hold the trumps because the rout of the NDA has left only one possible coalition open.

The verdict in West Bengal, Kerala and Tripura is even more remarkable in some ways. In West Bengal and Tripura, the contest was between the Left Front, the Trinamool Congress-led NDA and the Congress. In Kerala, it was largely between the Congress-led United Democratic Front (UDF) and the CPI (M)-

led Left Democratic Front (LDF). It was hardly a secret that in a post-poll scenario, the Congress and Left were likely to join hands to form a government in New Delhi if they had the numbers. The NDA tried to make much of this by pointing out that the battle between the Congress and the Left in these states was 'farcical' and amounted to not giving the voters a choice.

Again, the electorate seems to have recognized that in a coalition era it is quite possible that two parties are opposed to each other in specific states but are compelled to be on the same of the political divide at the federal level. Far from writing off the Left as the 'B team' of the Congress, the voters have given the Left more seats than it has ever had in the Lok Sabha.

Both political parties and analysts would do well to recognize that an electorate that was never politically naïve is becoming increasingly mature and sophisticated in exercising its franchise. The electorate is far more focused and certainly sure of what matters to their livelihood. In some cases, it has got ahead of the chatteratti. For the parties, such recognition is essential for survival, for the analysts it can help save them embarrassment in the future.

This is one story that most Indians prefer not to talk about and certainly not bring to the fore at a time when India's future is expected to look bright. But no can wish away the reality of poverty, unemployment and a suffering farm sector.

The reform process started in 1991 but tended to ignore India's huge agricultural economy. The recent growth levels of over 10.4 per cent has much to do with a good monsoon resulting in a better year for the farm sector and the farmers. Even the corporate sector realizes the significance of the farm sector as a good monsoon means a boost in consumption in rural India and the profits of this goes to the manufacturers of the produce. It may just be the right time to turn these areas of disturbance into spaces of opportunity that takes India's economy to another level.

The following essay throws light on the section of the have-nots and in a way suggests how large a market is being left out.

WAITING FOR THE SUN TO SHINE

Paranjoy Guha Thakurta

There are many in India who still scamper for food and who do not drink clean water, if they get any. There are thousands of farmers who committed suicide in recent years. Why? Because they were unable to repay loans. Why? Because their crops failed. Why? Because the monsoon played truant on their parched fields. Many pound the pathways of 'modern' urban India looking for jobs as the country's economy is supposed to be moving along at a pace that has surprised sections of Indians, not to mention the rest of the world.

Progress usually meant creation of jobs and reducing the gap between the rich and the poor. Economic reforms were not meant to focus on just a small section of society. Even after over a decade of so-called reforms, at least one out of four Indians somehow still manage to survive below the poverty line, any way you choose to draw it. The reforms process has hardly touched agriculture that contributes roughly a quarter of the country's gross domestic product (GDP) and provides direct and indirect livelihood to around two-thirds of the population. Jobless growth is a reality.

This chapter examines three interlinked aspects of the Indian reality: the farm sector, the incidence of poverty and employment.

Human Resource Development: An Uneven Picture

The National Human Development Report (NHDR) of the Government of India painted a rather mixed picture of the country. In many respects, the lot of the majority of one billion Indians is currently far better than what it used to be twenty years ago or even a decade earlier. At the same time, official indicators of human development show that economic and social progress has been unevenly spread across geographical areas.

Modelled along the lines of the global Human Development Report of the United Nations Development Programmes (UNDP), the 300-page official document — printed on glossy paper and released on April 23, 2002, by the then Prime Minister Atal Behari Vajpayee reveals (if one goes through the fine print) that the country still has a long way to go before the quality of life of a large proportion of its citizens improves significantly. At the all-India level, the improvement in the human development index (HDI) slowed down slightly — from a rate of growth of nearly twenty-six per cent in the 1980s to about twenty-four per cent in the 1990s.

On poverty, the report has pointed out that the share of the population living below the poverty line declined from nearly half (around forty-seven per cent) in the early 1980s to a little over a quarter (26 per cent) in 1999-2000. While conventional wisdom means defining poverty in terms of income or expenditure levels, in India, the Planning Commission defines poverty as the level of per head consumer expenditure that can provide an average daily intake of 2,400 calories per individual in rural areas and 2,100 calories per person in urban areas over and above a relatively small allocation of non-food items.

Using the internationally comparable estimate of the proportion of people living on less than US $ 1 a day as the poverty line (after adjusting for differences in purchasing power across countries), the decline in the proportion of the poor in

India was from around forty-six per cent in the early 1990s to thirty-nine per cent in 1999-2000. These figures should be considered in the context of the fact that India started the twenty-first century with a per capita income that was around half that of China and Indonesia — countries that were at comparable stages of development in the late 1960s and early '70s.

A UNDP report states that 223 million Indians go hungry to sleep, consuming less than 1,960 calories per day, despite the fact that the country is considered 'self-sufficient' in the production of wheat, rice and milk. What is appalling is that government agencies burn food stocks since these spoil in improper storage facilities. Food-for-work programmes are either not there or are not implemented in an efficient manner. And free distribution of food is hardly part of the system, although the need is glaring.

A 2003 report of the World Bank ("India: Sustaining Reform, Reducing Poverty") pointed out: "Growth has reduced poverty, but the pattern of growth was also decisive. Rural consumption growth reduced poverty in both rural and urban areas. Urban growth benefited the urban poor somewhat, but had no impact on rural poverty." The NHDR says: "the decline (in poverty) has been marginally more in rural areas... resulting in a narrowing down of the rural-urban gap." While the developmental distance between urban "India" and rural "Bharat" had come down somewhat, the inter-state differences in human poverty were "quite striking".

Social development is yet another issue that the nation is grappling with. According to the World Bank report quoted earlier: "Social progress in India has been uneven. Education indicators have improved markedly, but progress in health has been mixed. For the first time since Independence, the absolute number of illiterates in India declined between 1991 and 2001. Literacy rates, particularly for women. Enrolment rates of primary-age children rose and the gap in the enrolment ratios of boys and girls narrowed."

This sounds good on paper but not good enough. As Goldman Sachs[1] points out, "the demands of a growing work force will also fuel the need to fund education more effectively." It is further stated, "India's low levels of education, particularly at the secondary level, are a major obstacle to achieving long term growth potential."

Agriculture in India: Waiting for a Second Green Revolution

Former Prime Minister Lal Bahadur Shastri who succeeded India's first Prime Minister Jawaharlal Nehru in 1964 — had coined a famous slogan: 'Jai jawan, jai kisan' (Hail the soldier, hail the farmer). India had at that juncture just suffered a crippling loss in its conflict with China. The Green Revolution that transformed agriculture in large parts of northern India from the late 1960s onwards was yet to take place. Every political leader in India has subsequently sworn by Shastri's sentiments expressed in that evocative phrase.

[1] India: Realizing BRICs Potential, April 2004, Roopa Purushothanam.

Long before the BJP-led NDA government was voted out of power in May 2004, there were many who realized that much of India was not exactly shining, that substantial sections of the people were far from feeling good. None other than the then Deputy Prime Minister L. K. Advani had acknowledged that life may not be all that bright and glowing for many of the country's farmers. If, indeed, agriculture were prospering, former Finance Minister Jaswant Singh would not have gone out of his way to announce a slew of schemes aimed at redressing the genuine grievances of India's farmers earlier in the year in January and February.

Nor would the successor United Progressive Alliance government headed by Manmohan Singh have repeatedly emphasized the importance of improving the country's agriculture. As the common minimum programme drawn up by the centre-left coalition on May 27, 2004, stated: "The UPA government will ensure that public investment in agricultural research and extension, rural infrastructure and irrigation is stepped up in a significant manner at the very earliest."

There is more than enough official data available to indicate that Indian agriculture is not exactly in the pink of health, despite the high-pitched rhetoric about the need for a second 'green revolution'. A close perusal of official statistics would indicate that the real income earned by the average farmer in the country has actually come down by roughly ten per cent over the last seven years or thereabouts.

While the share of agriculture in gross domestic product has come down from over a quarter till the end of the 1990s to around twenty-two per cent at present, the farm sector continues to directly or indirectly provide a livelihood to close to two-thirds of India's population. One drought year (2002-03) and the index of agricultural production crashed by more than twelve per cent while production of foodgrain came down by around fourteen per cent. What has become rather apparent is that the country's agriculture is still far from having become immune to the whims of Lord Indra, the Hindu god of rainfall, although India has certainly come a long way since 1914 when the Royal Commission on Indian Currency and Finance under British rule described the budget as a 'gamble on the monsoon'.

The main reason why the farm sector was badly hit by the 2002-03 drought was a simple fact: only around forty per cent of the total cropped area in the country is irrigated. In other words, sixty per cent of the cropped area depends on the monsoon that runs its course between the months of June and September during which period more than three-fourths of the total annual precipitation takes place.

One does not have to learn about thousands of farmers committing suicide — while some of the huge stocks of wheat and rice in the godowns of the Food Corporation of India (FCI) are being eaten by rats and rodents — to realize that the so-called feel-good factor was non-existent amongst agricultural workers spread across the length and breadth of the country and even in relatively prosperous states like Punjab, Haryana, Uttar Pradesh and Andhra Pradesh. There is enough stated in the government's own documents that paint a rather dismal picture of Indian agriculture. But first, let us have a look at the positive side.

Among all countries in the world, India has the largest arable land area next only to the US. In terms of irrigated area, India is ranked first before the US. Given the incredibly wide variety of agro-climatic regions that exist in this country, it is hardly surprising that India produces almost all types of crops, fruits and vegetables that are grown on the planet — in tropical as well as temperate zones.

Through the decades of the 1960s, the 1970s and the 1980s, there was no dearth of doomsayers who predicted that India would not be able to feed her teeming millions. There were many who argued that what the British political economist Thomas Robert Malthus had claimed in 1798 in his *Essay on the Principle of Population*, would turn out to be correct as far as India was concerned. Malthus, who was well known for his pessimistic predictions on the future of humanity, had contended that while population would grow in geometric progression food output would increase in arithmetic progression — this imbalance would be rectified only by divine intervention in the form of famine and disasters, he believed.

The manner in which stocks of wheat and rice with the public sector FCI rose in recent years not merely disproved Malthus' worst apprehensions, the mountain of food-grain made the "ship-to-mouth" days of the 1960s seem like a distant nightmare. It was said that if each and every bag of grain were placed lengthwise, it would have traversed a distance all the way to the moon and back. Yet, the situation is far from hunky dory. The problem simply is that despite high stocks of wheat and rice, few can deny the fact that malnutrition is widespread in many parts of the country.

The annual rate of growth of production of all kinds of food-grain — wheat, rice, coarse cereals and pulses — stood at 1.67 per cent in the 1990s, a rate that was considerably lower than the rate of growth of population of 1.9 per cent during the decade. Why then have food stocks mounted so rapidly? The contradiction can be easily explained. First, the rate of growth of production of wheat and rice far outstripped the rate of population growth right through the 1980s after the much-talked-about Green Revolution. Secondly, the inclusion of pulses in the overall rate of growth of food output distorts the picture since production of pulses has been stagnant for over three decades resulting in a drop in per capita availability. Thirdly, coarse grains are being increasingly used to feed cattle and poultry. That's not all. There has been a distinct shift in consumer preferences towards non-cereal foods.

This fact only reflects how the farm sector is mismanaged. What would paint an even worse picture is the fact that the government spends more on stocking food grain than its entire Plan and non-Plan outlays on agriculture, rural development, irrigation and flood control! And yet food is not given out freely or even under a food-for-work programme.

At this point, India's farm sector is somewhat at a crossroads. As a member of the World Trade Organization (WTO), the Agreement on Agriculture is binding on India. The agreement provides for specific commitments by countries on steps that would improve market access to imported agricultural products and also bring down trade-distorting subsidies. For Indian farmers, the opening up of agricultural trade would imply that they would become more vulnerable to the impact of price fluctuations in the world market over which they would have no control. A reduction in domestic subsidies would increase costs of production while a reduction in export subsidies would make it that much more difficult for Indian farm produce to compete in international markets.

Obviously, the Indian farmer is handicapped on account of a variety of constraints, the most significant being the high product price, much above the international levels. While costs of cultivation per hectare are among the lowest in the world, so are yields thereby increasing product prices. Indian farmers find it profitable to export only during years when there has been a widespread crop failure resulting in prices going up. Farmers also miss out on opportunities in the food processing area as less than two per cent of the produce gets processed. As a result, the profits from this activity are small and not sufficient enough to reduce the prices of exportable items.

Further still, public investment is on the decline as share of investment in this sector has dropped from 1.6 per cent of the GDP in 1993-94, to 1.3 per cent in subsequent years. This has resulted in a slowdown in infrastructure building such as irrigation facilities that compensate to some extent for a poor monsoon.

The employment situation in agriculture is pretty pathetic. The *Economic Survey* for 2002-03 stated: "The decline in the overall growth rate of employment in 1994-2000 was largely attributable to a near stagnation of employment in agriculture. As a result, the share of agriculture in total employment dropped substantially from 60 per cent in 1993-94 to 57 per cent in 1999-2000." The same document for the previous year had pointed out that there had been a "significant structural change in the Indian economy" — the absolute number of persons employed in agriculture declined for the first time in the history of the country.

According to Abhijit Sen, professor of economics at Jawaharlal Nehru University and former chairman, CACP, the simplest fact about Indian agriculture at present is that available hard data shows that per capita agricultural output has been declining since 1996-97. There is strong evidence to suggest that the real income of each farmer in the country has actually come down by roughly ten per cent over the last seven years or so, he said in an interview with this writer.

The slowdown in the rate of growth of foodgrain output to below the rate of growth of population in the late-1990s caused considerable consternation about the country's food security. At the same time, India crossed the 200 million tonne mark in foodgrain output in this period. The ship-to-mouth situation is today considered a bad dream of the mid-1960s. Then came the 'green revolution', especially in Punjab, Haryana and west Uttar Pradesh. But the 'revolution' spread unevenly across the rest of the country. Even in India's 'granary', by the late-1980s, the limits of increasing farm productivity through the use of fertilisers, pesticides and high-yielding varieties of seeds, had been reached. In many rice-growing areas in particular, a high crop yield remained elusive.

Many economists have an almost blind faith in the belief that one index of how quickly a country develops is how fast the share of agriculture in the national income comes down. This trend is apparent in India as well. Still, there remain crucial questions concerning the long-term performance of the country's farmers.

When would India's poor earn enough, that is, possess adequate entitlement or purchasing power to obtain sufficient quantities of food to feed themselves and their families? How should available land be better distributed without fragmentation of farm holdings resulting in productivity stagnating or declining? How should food storage systems be improved to reduce wastage, to prevent rats and rodents from eating up grain and to check 'two-legged' rodents from stealing the produce? How should intermediaries be made less exploitative and more efficient to reduce the wide gap in the prices at which farmers sell their crop and the prices at which consumers purchase? How long can various state governments — including those of agriculturally better-off states, continue to provide subsidised (or free) power to all categories of farmers, small and big, wealthy and poor? And, for how long could the wealthy strawberry-grower of, say, Punjab, earning a profit of Rs 1,50,000 per month continue to remain outside the net of the income tax department?

The manner in which India tackles these crucial issues would, to a considerable extent, determine whether the farm sector would continue to remain as strong as it is.

Table 3
Index of Agricultural Production (% change)

	1997-98	1998-99	1999-2000	2000-01	2001-02	2002-03	2003-04 Projected
Agriculture production	-5.7	8.1	-0.5	-6.6	7.2	-12.5	13.8
Foodgrains	-3.1	6.1	2.7	-6.7	8.4	-14.6	14.2
Non-foodgrains	-9.2	10.4	-4.8	-6.4	5.3	-9.3	13.1

Unemployment in India: Jobless Growth

There is one word that was missing from much of the debate and discussion on current economic issues during the 1990s. The word is 'employment'. Economic analysts had frequently discussed different aspects of globalization, liberalization, privatization, divestment and so on but relatively few had laid much emphasis on the issue of employment that used to dominate the discourse on economics in India right through the first four decades after Independence.

The fact of the matter is that the employment scenario in the country right now is pretty bleak and there are no signs of any improvement. A large section of India's youth faces a jobless future. One does not have to search very far but look at the official *Economic Survey* to confirm one's worst apprehensions. It has been pointed out that the "decline in the rate of growth of employment in the 1990s was associated with a comparatively higher growth rate in GDP, indicating a decline in the labour intensity of production". The 55th round of the quinquennial survey of the National Sample Survey Organisation has stated that the annual rate of growth of employment declined from 2.7 per cent between 1983 and 1993-4 to a mere 1.07 per cent between 1993-94 and 1999-2000. During these two periods, the overall rate of growth of population came down from 2 per cent per year to 1.95 per cent.

The employment elasticity of output declined from 0.52 to 0.16 between these two periods. This decline cut across virtually all sectors of the economy — there was a near stagnation of employment in agriculture in the second half of the 1990s — the exceptions being transport, financial services and real estate. Shorn of jargon, what is apparent is that while the rate of growth of population in India has come down, the number of new jobs created in the economy has declined even faster because of the growing use of capital-intensive technologies.

Data available from 939 employment exchanges in the country indicate that at the end of September last year, the number of job-seekers (all of whom are not necessarily unemployed) stood at 41.6 million, of which roughly 70 per cent were educated up to at least the 10th standard. According to statistics compiled by the Directorate General of Employment and Training in the Ministry of Labour, the total employment in the public sector came down for the fifth year in succession: from 19.56 million at the end of March 1997 to 19.14 million in 2001.

The loss of jobs in the public sector was hardly compensated by growth of employment opportunities in the private sector. Employment in the organised private sector came down from 8.75 million in 1998 to 8.65 million two years later. If there was any consolation, it was the creation of 6000 jobs in the organized private sector, but that's hardly a thrill.

Those who are optimistic believe that the number of self-employed would grow significantly in the years ahead as more people shun contractual jobs with uncertain short tenures. What has taken place for the first time in the country is that the absolute number of persons engaged in agriculture has declined, last year's *Economic Survey* had stated. Should one be surprised then that phrases like 'economic liberalisation' or 'second-generation reforms' fail to excite those outside the corridors of chambers of commerce and apex industry associations like the Confederation of Indian Industry (CII) and

Federation of Indian Chambers of Commerce and Industry (FICCI)?

The late Pravin Visaria was among the authors of a study (published in *Twenty-first Century India*, Oxford University Press, 2004) that categorically stated that "economic growth by itself is not the answer to India's future employment scenario".

As more and more entrepreneurs talk of lean production, re-engineering, total quality management and 'decruiting', workers are becoming increasingly uncertain about the future. In his book entitled *End of Work* (Penguin, 2000), author Jeremy Rifkin has detailed instances of how young people the world over are giving vent to their frustration and rage by anti-social behaviour while older individuals, "caught between a prosperous past and a bleak future", feel trapped by social forces over which they have little or no control.

"While earlier industrial technologies replaced the physical power of human labour, substituting machines for body and brawn, the new computer-based technologies promise a replacement of the human mind itself, substituting thinking machines for human beings across the entire gamut of economic activity," Rifkin has written. Life as we know it, is being altered in fundamental ways, he has added. Millions the world over had placed their hopes for a better tomorrow on the liberating potential of the computer revolution. Yet, as Rifkin points out, the truth is that in India and the world over, the economic fortunes of most working people continue to deteriorate amid the embarrassment of technological riches the benefits of which reach only the elite and in India, that number is a small percentage of its population.

The truth is that poverty and the development of human resource, the problems of the farm sector and unemployment are issues that are as real as India's progress in the information technology sector and in complete contrast of the living style of urban Indians. While India may be thrilled that this is the youngest nation, the point is that without broad-based progress, the additional annual labour force of an estimated nine million would grow old experiencing poverty rather than prosperity through employment.

The translation of an ancient Sanskrit couplet runs:

> "My best respects to poverty
> The master who has set me free
> For I can look at all the world
> And no one looks at me."

I disagree completely with the sentiments expressed. Why should the poor be meek and submissive and not protest against inequality and injustice? Unless India's inequalities in terms of social and economic classes narrow considerably, the country would not be able to develop faster nor move ahead in the international arena, certainly not fast enough. Many of the non-economic divisions in Indian society would conceivably become less oppressive if the economic divide is reduced.

If better education and health-care improves the quality of life and productivity of India's vast human resources, it would almost invariably improve the effective and sustainable utilisation of the country's other resources, particularly natural resources. The indiscriminate manner in which the Indian elite has squandered the bounties of nature — water, land, forests, minerals and wildlife — cannot obviously continue. The empowerment of hitherto suppressed sections of society could stall such regression, hopefully reverse it.

The crucial issue for India's future is whether the country's leaders would be able to bargain better with giant global corporate conglomerates to protect the country's natural resources and the interests of the weak and the vulnerable. The problem has been the collective inability of the peoples of this vast and diverse nation to first identify and then marginalise the traitors in our midst, those who had cheaply bartered away national economic interests for private profit.

INDIA AT THE
ARRIVAL LOUNGE

There are all kinds of punctuations in India, but as the title of Mark Tully's book said, there are 'no full stops in India.' It is a constant evolution, so at times an assumed full stop is not really one, as it may just be a slow down after a quick run. The contrast at times can transmit a feeling of stagnation and a lack of flow, but not a full stop. That India has a long away to go after a long way coming makes sure that there are no such finalities.

So while this book comes to a close, the realization of what India is does not, it is an on-going process. This book gives you a glimpse of only what the India brand stands for today.

As these lines are keyed in, a report in *The Economic Times* states that as many 210 companies turned their fortunes around during the past year[1], notching up profits.

Industry, at the beginning of the Indian financial year, April, has recorded high growth levels of 9.4 per cent and for the period till June 2004, it has clocked a 7.4 per cent of growth. The manufacturing sector is on the fast track and electricity consumption has also been higher than what it was April 2003, indicating increased industrial consumption—a sign of growth. And this is substantiated by the increased profitability of corporate India. Net profit of industry is up by 30 per cent for the June quarter![2] Exports are also up at almost 26 per cent till June and a report[3] suggests that the top 100 Indian corporates have posted a 35 per cent rise in export turnover.

---

[1] *The Economic Times*, 'India Inc out of woods puts up a fighting score' by Vijay Gurav & Daniel Fernandes, June 11, 2004.

[2] *The Economic Times*, 'India Inc net up 30% at Rs 20,000 crore in June qtr', by Rajas Kelkar, August 1, 2004.

[3] *The Economic Times*, 'Top 100 cos post 35% rise in export turnover', by Vijay Gurav & Daniel Fernandes, August 1, 2004.

Another report[4] suggests that the opposition in the US against outsourcing may just be losing steam. The US labour department has shown that the outsourced jobs to other countries is not a huge number or the prime cause for unemployment — India's contention for a long time now. And an AT Kearney report released in October 2004 places India at number three among FDI distinction.

These news reports and developments tie in with the affirmation of India's changing position locally as well as globally. But it also reflects the great divide within India that of the progressing and of those being left behind. There are no convincing positive reports suggesting that India's farm sector is even close to solving any of its problems. What has hit the papers during the recent past is yet again death of farmers in Andhra Pradesh and starvation in West Bengal.

The World Bank in its report says "Sustained progress will no doubt be difficult, especially in the politically charged areas of labour, power and agricultural reforms. But it also promises high returns be reducing poverty."[5] This conclusive remark highlights the challenges and the results of trying to overcome them.

Significantly, the current UPA government led by the Congress has clearly spelt out an amended reforms agenda that focuses on the agricultural sector, starvation, poverty, unemployment—all areas of concern that if not addressed can pull the country back from greater levels of growth if not addressed. According to Ruchir Sharma of Morgan Stanley, a lot would depend on "how focused the political class is. Indian standards are still set a bit too low that of seven to nine per cent growth. There are many unproductive areas that need to be tapped. Once the economy is more broad based, then we could surpass the set targets and sustain much higher levels of growth."

---

[4] *The Economic Times*, 'US wakes up to fact: India does not steal jobs', June 12, 2004.
[5] World Bank Report, India: Sustaining Reform, Reducing Poverty.

Political will is always an issue and the World Bank report quoted earlier mentions that in its own way. However, the current government has come into power with an objective of giving the reforms breadth in definition and depth in terms of impact. The finance minister, P. Chidambaram has expressed the government's willingness to increase investments in the laggard areas of agriculture and education. At the same time, the prosperous parts of India would not be neglected indicating that an environment for increased foreign direct investment (FDI) will not be ignored, he has said. And this is reflected in his budget announcement to increase FDI in sectors such as banking, telecom and civil aviation. The role of non-resident Indians (NRIs) is also expected to be crucial and for the first time, there is a department at the Centre that will focus on this group that have been an integral part of the new India script. India's focus, it would appear, is borrowed from China that has benefited by huge investments from their expatriates.

Policies aside, if there is an issue of concern, it is of money and implementation—the latter being possibly as crucial as the former as India has had a history of misuse of funds and the lack of accountability.

While the finance minister made the right noises, the task before him is not all that easy unless his colleagues at the Centre decide to cuts the red tape in the system. "Work done by the World Bank shows that it takes 88 days to start a business in India, twice the regional average," and "it takes almost twice as long to close a business in India."[6] If the investment environment has to change, addressing the administrative set up is the trigger.

A hurdle-ridden system or the red tape as pointed out earlier, would discourage foreign investors that could result in more and more dependence on government funding, an

---

[6] Goldman Sachs, Global Economic Paper 109, 'India: Realizing BRICs Potential'.

increased fiscal deficit, higher levels of inflation and less cash for the private sector. And this could become a worrisome issue given the need for a fresh thrust in building infrastructure and improving the education system.

According to Goldman Sachs, in the immediate term (projects already identified by the previous government) almost US $150 billion is needed in some significant infrastructure projects that are linked with irrigation and the farm sector, trade and tourism and railways. Of this amount, US $122 billion is needed for the river-linking project that would "resolve the problem of drought in rain deficient areas, generation of hydro power and effective use of rain water." A ten to twelve year project according to GS, it can solve a number of problems for the farm sector and industry. Poverty levels could drop, employment could increase and the dependence on the vagaries of weather would reduce. Besides, a prospering rural class and increasing middle level in the nation would mean greater demand from the corporate sector.

Can this happen? The expectations of India globally and the pressures from these quarters and a demanding domestic set up can push the governments into a developmental mode without closing is doors to the openness it needs in terms of trade and investments.

India's economic reform measures have worked even if for a certain class or for a few classes. The urban middle class is increasing in size as I write; it currently numbers 300 million people and is expected to rise to 445 million by the end of 2006. Where were they before they became part of this segment? This is anyone's guess. But most likely, the same people were aspiring and striving to get there. No economist, irrespective of their ideological leaning can deny that. This data indicates that the reforms as chaotic as it has been over the past decade and more, has yielded results. If a more collective approach is in place, then who knows, Goldman Sachs' BRIC report may well turn out to be a reality — India could be the third largest economy in less than fifty years.

It is projected that income levels will double every ten years. Within a generation, almost fifty per cent of India's people could become middle-class and poverty could diminish to fifteeen per cent.

But to bring more of India in to this better-off or well-to-do segment, calls for investments, as pointed out earlier.

India is in the limelight but that is not enough. The performance so far and particularly recently, has meant greater expectation. What is needed is not a nimble foot but a firm step forward that suggests that the Indian mind and body are both moving with less hesitation. World Banks 'Doing Business in 2005' report released in September 2004 states that India made the most progress among South Asian nations in improving its investment climate and is among the top ten reformers for 2003. However, the same report had little to say about the ease of doing business in the country.

What could force mindsets to change, however, more than the change in thinking in 1991 (opening up of the Indian economy) is the youthfulness of the Indian population. Over the past five to six years, the younger Indian has shown a greater level of confidence and knowledge than ever before. The new young Indian is coming from a position of 'strength' despite all the country's shortcomings, and is not prepared to compromise on his rights or expectations. He is prepared to stand toe-to-toe and battle it out with competition.

This is being reflected in our knowledge economy, sportsmen, writers, entrepreneurs and in cultural issues such as taboo themes in movies, theatre and the paint and sketches on canvasses. While undoubtedly the reference here is to a very small number of Indians, the magnitude of the story in other parts of the country could only be larger and the impact even greater.

What the youth does is speed up things due to their adaptability to newer technologies. The adaptability of the younger lot could be seen even in remote parts of Karnataka where Thomas L. Friedman in an article[7] had pointed out he was out paced by a young 'untouchable' girl at speed typing! He had been typing for many years more than her age. She was just an eight-year-old.

The e-chaupal (IT-based retailing system) programme involving farmers is an indication of this change.

The response to the 'India Shining' campaign is yet another indication that the Indians are more aware than one may think them to be. They are evolving nearly as fast as available technology.

This pace could be the new age challenge for politicians – where the demands from the young would mean quick supply. The dynamics of the situation would be such that while votes from the rural and urban may come based on promises to give power, jobs and education over the next ten years (without delivering), pure economic consumption and the country's international public relations will come from the informed lot of urbanites, who will demand power at economic rates.

One would ask then, who should be leading India. The elections of 2004 showed Indians voting in all of the young first timers, be they from the Congress, BJP or any other political party. And significantly, they talked of the same issues – unemployment, growth, prosperity, poverty and rural development. The distinction from the elders though was the suggested use of technology. They may explain that while there is only a single youngster in the council of ministers, Dayanidhi Maran, he was been put in charge of the IT and communications ministries.

The profile of the younger Indian in India's growth path is bound to change. They come with less baggage of the old school of thought where religion, caste and gender biases were almost an integral part of growing up. The recent uproar against a change in dress code disallowing western clothing in certain

---

[7] The IHT Online, Thomas L. Friedman: A Lesson in India, May 21, 2004.

educational institutes in Madhya Pradesh, is an indication of the way the young respond today. The acceptance of the woman is greater among the youth and discriminations of any kind are significantly lower. If anything matters to them, it is employment, prosperity and the 'cash in hand'.

"The youth has been one of the key drivers in India. This is explained in the speedy growth in sales of mobile sets. The BOP call center business has resulted in more cash in the hands of the young who are ready to spend more freely than other generations. This generation is ready to fly across the globe, are ready to explore and present themselves as positive brand ambassadors," says Farokh Balsara, a partner at Ernst and Young's Mumbai office in India.

True. But they can't solve all of India's problems.

The Indian economy and industry seems to be moving away from the typical manufacturing industry and there is some amount of insecurity coming from missing the industrial revolution. Academic, Shiv Visvanathan comments that the problem with many of India's institutions of higher learning are that these have become transformed into the intellectual assembly lines of the world, clearing houses for ideas, both good and bad, which the world gratefully accepts or summarily rejects. This, indeed, is paradoxically India's biggest strength and her biggest weakness.

This paradox does create uncertainty and insecurity given that India seems to be skipping the industrial revolution. The manufacturing sector is important but is not expected to be the prime creator of jobs. It is the failure of farm sector reforms that has led to an inflated labour class in urban India that cannot be absorbed by industry. And for the services sector, basic education and skills is a necessity.

So what is required is a right mix.

The former prime minister, Atal Behari Vajpayee at a rally in the run up to the 2004 general elections said that India had announced its arrival on the world stage "of an India that will be an economic powerhouse and a land of opportunity and achievement". The Congress leader, Sonia Gandhi suggested the opposite and accused the government of selective development where slums made way for call centers, technology parks and shopping malls white ignoring India's large population living in the uncertainties of the nation's agriculture sector.[8]

None of the leaders were wrong in their assumptions, accusations and pronouncements.

India needs to be both, developed in the urban parts and not backward in the rural regions of the country.

There is no doubt that every region will evolve in its own way. While economic and related material aspirations may differ, that should not be an allowance to let poverty levels rise. By the same token, it must be understood that the job at hand is not an overnight task. Metro cities in India would continue to have shantytowns but the difference could be that the inhabitants would get more than a square meal and sufficient education to be aware and know his rights. Rural India would have to wait till infrastructure projects are completed to realize a better life that gives everyone sufficient comfort to tap their potential.

What is wished for and hoped for is that every Indian one day would wake up and see the sun shine. Every drop of rain should drench them with prosperity and happiness. There is no better realization than this.

---

[8] *Time Asia* (on the net), 'Subcontinental Divide', Alex Perry, February 23, 2004.

ABOUT THE CONTRIBUTORS

Roopa Purushothanam, is the economist who shot to fame after authoring the Goldman Sachs BRIC reports in October 2003 and April 2004.

R. Venkatraman, is executive director, KPMG India and head of the firm's IT cell.

Govindraj Ethiraj, CNBC-TV 18's Corporate Editor is a regular commentator on India's corporate sector.

Dr. Narendra Pani, senior editor with *The Economic Times*, Bangalore, is a close follower of India's trade sector and its international trade relations.

Abheek Barman, is an editor with *The Times of India*, New Delhi, and has been teaching the Indian economy and reform process even during his ten year stint with *The Economic Times*.

Khozem Merchant, *Financial Times'* Mumbai bureau correspondent, has been covering Indian industry and its relevance in the international media.

Pallavi Aiyar, is a freelance journalist in Beijing, and has been producing reports for TV and print media in India.

Shibu Itty Kuttickal, is a senior journalist working with *Today* in Singapore. He was formerly with *Khaleej Times* in Dubai and other publications in India.

Vivek Rai, is a freelance journalist living in New York. He worked as a broadcast news reporter for seven years in India, and now produces reports for TV, print and the net.

Ben King, is a writer, journalist and confirmed Indophile, based in London. His work has appeared in *The Financial Times*, the *Mail On Sunday*, and a range of other newspapers and magazines.

Santosh Desai, president McCann Erickson's India office, is a frequent commentator on the Indian advertising market and its relevance in the social space.

Rumy M. Narayan, a freelance writer, has been researching India's retail market for several years.

Malavika Sangghvi, is editor of *The Times of India's* Sunday Special – Men & Women.

R. Shankar, is a freelance writer and commentator on India's voting patterns, electorate and political process.

Paranjoy Guha Thakurta, a commentator on India's economy, has been a journalist for over twenty years and is now executive director of the School Of Convergence in New Delhi.

2